AUGUST WILSON

in an hour

BY JOAN HERRINGTON

SUSAN C. MOORE, SERIES EDITOR

PLAYWRIGHTS in an hour
know the playwright, love the play

IN AN HOUR BOOKS • HANOVER, NEW HAMPSHIRE • INANHOURBOOKS.COM
AN IMPRINT OF SMITH AND KRAUS PUBLISHERS, INC • SMITHANDKRAUS.COM

With grateful thanks to Carl R. Mueller,
whose fascinating introductions to his translations of the Greek and
German playwrights provided inspiration for this series.

Published by In an Hour Books
an imprint of Smith and Kraus, Inc.
177 Lyme Road, Hanover, NH 03755
inanhourbooks.com SmithandKraus.com

Know the playwright, love the play.

In an Hour, In a Minute, and Theater IQ are registered trademarks of
In an Hour Books.

© 2009 by In an Hour Books
All rights reserved
Manufactured in the United States of America
First edition: April 2010
10 9 8 7 6 5 4 3 2 1

FENCES. © 1986 by August Wilson. Used by permission of Dutton Signet, a division of
Penguin Group (USA), Inc.
GEM OF THE OCEAN. © 2003, 2006 by August Wilson. Used by permission of Theatre
Communications Group.
JOE TURNER'S COME AND GONE. © 1988 by August Wilson. Used by permission of The-
atre Communications Group.
KING HEDLEY II. © 1997 by the estate of August Wilson. Used by permission of Theatre
Communications Group.
TWO TRAINS RUNNING. © 1992 by August Wilson. Used by permission of Dutton, a divi-
sion of Penguin Group (USA), Inc.

Front cover design by Dan Mehling, dmehling@gmail.com
Text design by Kate Mueller, Electric Dragon Productions
Book production by Dede Cummings Design, DCDesign@sover.net

ISBN-13: 978-1-936232-33-8
ISBN-10: 1-936232-33-2
Library of Congress Control Number: 2009943236

CONTENTS

Why Playwrights in an Hour?

This new series by Smith and Kraus Publishers titled Playwrights in an Hour has a dual purpose for being: one academic, the other general. For the general reader, this volume, as well as the many others in the series, offers in compact form the information needed for a basic understanding and appreciation of the works of each volume's featured playwright. Which is not to say that there don't exist volumes on end devoted to each playwright under consideration. But inasmuch as few are blessed with enough time to read the splendid scholarship that is available, a brief, highly focused accounting of the playwright's life and work is in order. The central feature of the series, a thirty- to forty-page essay, integrates the playwright into the context of his or her time and place. The volumes, though written to high standards of academic integrity, are accessible in style and approach to the general reader as well as to the student and, of course, to the theater professional and theatergoer. These books will serve for the brushing up of one's knowledge of a playwright's career, to the benefit of theater work or theatergoing. The Playwrights in an Hour series represents all periods of Western theater: Aeschylus to Shakespeare to Wedekind to Ibsen to Williams to Beckett, and on to the great contemporary playwrights who continue to offer joy and enlightenment to a grateful world.

Carl R. Mueller
School of Theater, Film and Television
Department of Theater
University of California, Los Angeles

Introduction

The seeds of August Wilson's theatrical development were planted in the radical years surrounding and following the assassinations of Martin Luther King (1968) and Malcolm X (1965). First, Leroi Jones' (later Amiri Baraka's) contribution of two inflammatory Off-Broadway plays, *Dutchman* and *The Slave* (1964), signaled the presence of a rebellious new black voice on stage. Then, James Baldwin, a novelist and essayist, demonstrated with *Blues for Mister Charlie* (1964) that he had playwriting instincts, too. And finally a large number of African-American dramatists, among them Lonnie Elder, OyomO, Ed Bullins, and others began to investigate an African-American culture that for years had been kept in the shadows.

But nothing had prepared this country for the entrance of August Wilson — born Frederick August Kittel in the Hill District of Pittsburgh. Beginning as a poet, inspired by Bessie Smith and the racking pain of the blues, Wilson delivered his first major work with *Ma Rainey's Black Bottom* in 1984. Other plays had preceded it, but this Broadway hit was the first to receive national attention. Soon, Wilson embarked upon a ten-play series of work, later known as The Pittsburgh Cycle, designed to celebrate the black experience in every decade of the twentieth century. These works varied in quality from the highly charged, poetic *Joe Turner's Come and Gone* to the less successful *Radio Golf*. It was an incredibly ambitious effort, matched only in size and audacity by Eugene O'Neill's projected (but unfinished) cycle of plays about the entire American historical experience. O'Neill had intended an eleven-play chronicle of an Irish-American family. He only wrote two — *A Touch of the Poet* and the unfinished *More Stately Mansions*. Unlike O'Neill, Wilson in fact finished his cycle of ten plays about the African-American experience before he died.

As the country's leading black playwright, collecting one Tony and two Pulitzer Prizes, Wilson began to function as a spokesman for the African-American theater as a whole. In a highly publicized event at

Town Hall, he and I debated whether color-blind casting is an aberrant idea. Wilson encouraged white directors to refrain from staging black playwright's plays. Wilson also criticized the current process — of which he was perhaps the greatest beneficiary — of cycling black plays through "white" theaters instead of originating them in black-run institutions.

Positions such as these were perhaps related to the fact that Wilson was half white himself. His father had been an immigrant German baker. In a well-publicized speech, he asserted that the "ground on which I stand" was the deck of a seventeenth-century slave ship. Clearly, that ground also included the floor of a twentieth-century German bakeshop. If Wilson had lived longer, he might have reexamined these inconsistencies, especially in the light of the Obama election, and perhaps evolved a more consistent take on the relations between the black and white people of America. Alas, we'll never know. He died too soon, but not before creating a body of work that was electrifying in its plotting, majestic in its sweep, syncopated in its rhythms, powerful in its characters, and awe-inspiring in its ambitions.

Robert Brustein
Founding director of the Yale and American Repertory Theatres
Distinguished Scholar in Residence, Suffolk University

A. Wilson

IN A MINUTE

AGE	YEAR	
–	1945	**Enter Frederick August Kittell (aka August Wilson), on April 27.**
2	1947	Jackie Robinson breaks the color line in major league baseball.
3	1948	Alan Payton — *Cry the Beloved Country*
6	1951	*I Love Lucy* arrives on TV sets.
8	1953	Arthur Miller — *The Crucible*
9	1954	Brown v. Board of Ed outlaws segregation.
14	1959	Lorraine Hansberry — *A Raisin in the Sun*
17	1962	Adolf Eichmann is captured by Israelis in Argentina.
18	1963	Martin Luther King Jr.'s "I Have a Dream" speech inspires America.
19	1964	Heavyweight champion Cassius Clay joins Nation of Islam, becomes Mohammed Ali.
		LeRoi Jones — *The Dutchman, The Slave*
20	1965	Malcolm X is assassinated by Black Muslims.
22	1967	Negro Ensemble Company is founded.
25	1970	The National Guard fires on students at Kent State; four students are killed.
27	1972	The Temptations' "Papa Was a Rollin' Stone" tops the charts.
28	**1973**	**August Wilson — *Recycle***
37	**1982**	**August Wilson — *Jitney***
39	**1984**	**August Wilson — *Ma Rainey's Black Bottom***
41	**1986**	**August Wilson — *Fences***
42	**1987**	**August Wilson — *Joe Turner's Come and Gone***
43	1988	Toni Morrison — *Beloved*
44	1989	Playwright Vaclav Havel elected president of Czechoslovakia.
46	**1991**	**August Wilson — *Two Trains Running***
49	1994	UN ignores Rwandan genocide. Nelson Mandela becomes president of South Africa.
50	**1995**	**August Wilson — *Seven Guitars***
51	1996	Harold Pinter — *Ashes to Ashes*
53	1998	Al Qaeda attacks U.S. embassies in Tanzania and Kenya; mostly Africans were victimized.
54	**1999**	**August Wilson — *King Hedley II***
58	**2003**	**August Wilson — *Gem of the Ocean***
59	2004	Sen. Barak Obama gives rousing keynote address at Democratic Convention.
60	**2005**	**Exit August Wilson, August 2.**

A snapshot of the playwright's world. From historical events to pop-culture and the literary landscape of the time, this brief list catalogues events that directly or indirectly impacted the playwright's writing. Play citations refer to premiere dates.

A. Wilson

DRAMATIC WORKS

Recycle

The Janitor

The Homecoming

Coldest Day of the Year

Fullerton Street

Black Bart and the Sacred Hills

Jitney

Ma Rainey's Black Bottom

Fences

Joe Turner's Come and Gone

The Piano Lesson

Two Trains Running

Seven Guitars

King Hedley II

Gem of the Ocean

Radio Golf

PUBLISHED POETRY

"Bessie." In *Black Lines* (summer 1971): 68.

"Testimonies." In *Antaeus* 66 (spring 1991): 474–79.

ESSAYS AND ARTICLES

"August Wilson Responds." *American Theatre*, October 1996: 105–107.

"Characters Behind History Teach Wilson About Plays." *New York Times*,
April 12, 1992, sec. H5.

This section presents a complete list of the playwright's works in chronological order by date written.

Foreword to *Romare Bearden: His Life and Art,* edited by Myron Schwartzman. New York: Harry N. Abrams, 1990.

"The Ground on Which I Stand." Keynote address to the Theatre Communications Group, June 26, 1996. *American Theatre* 13, no. 7 (1996): 14–17, 71–74.

"How to Write a Play Like August Wilson." *New York Times*, March 10, 1991, sec. 2.5, 17.

"I Want a Black Director." In *May All Your Fences Have Gates,* edited by Alan Nadel. Iowa City: University of Iowa Press, 1994.

Introduction to *Romance, Rhythm and Revolution: Selected Poetry of Rob Penny.* Magnolia Press, 1990. ISBN 0929917006.

"The Legacy of Malcolm X." *Life,* December 1992, 84–94.

"Living on Mother's Prayer." *New York Times*, May 12, 1996, sec. 4.13.

Preface to *August Wilson: Three Plays.* Pittsburgh: University of Pittsburgh Press, 1991.

Onstage with A. Wilson

Introducing Colleagues and
Contemporaries of August Wilson

 THEATER

Edward Albee, American playwright

Amiri Baraka, American playwright and poet

Ed Bullins, American playwright

Alice Childress, American playwright

Michael Feingold, American critic and dramaturge

Arthur Miller, American playwright

Tennessee Williams, American playwright

George C. Wolfe, American director and playwright

 ARTS

John Cage, American composer

Merce Cunningham, American dancer

Philip Glass, American composer

Robert Frank, Swiss-born photographer

John Barks "Dizzy" Gillespie, American jazz musician

Jackson Pollock, American painter

Bessie Smith, American blues singer

The Temptations, American "Motown" band

 FILM

Woody Allen, American filmmaker

Richard Burton, Welsh actor

James Earl Jones, American actor

This section lists contemporaries whom the playwright may or may not have known.

Spike Lee, American filmmaker
Sidney Poitier, American actor
Phylicia Rashad, American actress
Martin Scorsese, American filmmaker
Sala Udin, American actor

POLITICS/MILITARY

Medgar Evers, American civil rights activist
Louis Farrakhan, American head of the Nation of Islam
Jesse Jackson, American minister and civil rights advocate
Lyndon B. Johnson, American president
Nelson Mandela, South African activist and president
Colin Powell, American, former secretary of state
Osama bin Laden, Saudi Arabian Islamic militant terrorist
Harmond Wilks, American, first black mayor of Pittsburgh

SCIENCE

Patricia Bath, American inventor
Emmett Chappelle, American bacteriologist
Paul Farmer, American doctor and public health advocate
Stephen Jay Gould, American paleontologist
John Forbes Nash, American mathematician and economist
Samuel Massie, American chemist
Edward Teller, American atomic scientist
James Watson, American biochemist

LITERATURE

Maya Angelou, American author and poet
Saul Bellow, American novelist
Jorge Luis Borges, Argentinean author
W. E. B. Du Bois, American author, poet, and scholar
Henry Louis Gates, American literary critic

John Updike, American author
Alice Walker, American author
Richard Wright, American author

RELIGION/PHILOSOPHY
Billy Graham, American evangelist
Ayatollah Ruhollah Khomeini, Iranian Mullah
Martin Luther King, American civil rights leader
Dalai Lama, spiritual leader of Tibet, Nobel Peace Prize laureate
Elijah Muhammad, American founder of the Nation of Islam
Richard John Neuhaus, Canadian-American Catholic thinker
Sayyid Qutb, Egyptian Islamist
Mother Theresa, Albanian-born Roman Catholic nun

SPORTS
Muhammad Ali, American boxer
Arthur Ashe, American tennis player
Jim Brown, American football player
Althea Gibson, American tennis player
Magic Johnson, American basketball player
Willie Mays, American baseball player
Tommie Smith, American Olympic gold-medalist
Tiger Woods, American golfer

INDUSTRY/BUSINESS
Shawn "Jay Z" Carter, American music producer
George Foreman, American entrepreneur and pugilist
Milton Freedman, American economist
Allan Greenspan, American Federal Reserve chairman
Earl G. Graves Sr., American founder of *Black Enterprise*
Andy Grove, Hungarian-American, a founder of Intel
Michael Milkin, American financier
Muhammad Yunus, Bangladeshi banker, Nobel laureate

A. WILSON

in an hour

Only when lions have historians will hunters cease being victims.
(African proverb)

From the deep and the near South the sons and daughters of newly freed African slaves wander into the city. Isolated, cut off from memory, having forgotten the names of the gods and only guessing at their faces, they arrive dazed and stunned, their hearts kicking in their chests with a song worth singing. They arrive carrying Bibles and guitars, their pockets lined with dust and fresh hope, marked men and women seeking to scrape from the narrow, crooked cobbles and the fiery blasts of the coke furnace a way of bludgeoning and shaping the malleable parts of themselves into a new identity as free men of definite and sincere worth.

Foreigners in a strange land, they carry as part and parcel of their baggage a long line of separation and dispersement which informs their sensibilities and marks their conduct as they search for ways to reconnect, to reassemble, to give clear and luminous meaning

---

This is the core of the book. The essay places the playwright in the context of his or her world and analyzes the influences and inspirations within that world.

1

to the song which is both a wail and a whelp of joy. (Prologue to *Joe Turner's Come and Gone*)

Before his early death in 2005, August Wilson had chronicled the history of African Americans by creating a play for each decade of this century; he provided a sustained and profound dramatic embodiment of the African-American experience, which he described in a 1994 unpublished interview with this author as "the dramatic tracing of the Black American odyssey." In the prologue to *Joe Turner's Come and Gone*, above, August Wilson describes the fundamental challenge he chose to confront as a playwright — the fortification of a people who have been disconnected from their cultural past.

However far a stream flows, it never forgets its origin.

Time after time, throughout his life, when August Wilson stood on a corner in the Hill District of Pittsburgh, his face lit up. He pointed to the apartment houses, the diners, the backyards where his plays are set. He stood on a corner where he listened to the voices of those who people his dramas. He was refueled by his childhood neighborhood.

Frederick August Kittel was born in 1945, the fourth of six children. His father, whose name he had been given, was a German immigrant. His mother was an African-American cleaning woman, Daisy Wilson. Daisy Wilson had come from the South. She and her mother had walked from North Carolina to Pennsylvania to start a new life. But her marriage did not work out as she had planned. According to Wilson, his father, Frederick Kittel, did not maintain much of a presence in the two-room apartment above the grocery store where they lived. It was a poor neighborhood populated with African Americans and with Jewish and Italian immigrants.

Despite his mixed heritage, Daisy's son identified with his mother, and his identity was formed in the fires of racism. When Daisy Wilson won a radio contest with a new Speed Queen washing machine as the prize, the family was elated. But when the station found out she was black, they refused to provide the new machine and instead offered a used one. Daisy Wilson turned it down, telling her son, "Something is not always better than nothing."

But "something" was getting harder and harder to find in the Hill District, as Daisy Wilson and her children witnessed. The Hill District had seen its heyday. The area had become a cultural hotspot in the 1930s, and until the 1950s was one of the most prosperous and influential black neighborhoods in the United States. The Hill had jazz legends, well-known writers, and the Pittsburgh Crawfords, a baseball team that played in the Negro National League with such players as Satchel Paige and Josh Gibson. Claude McKay, the Harlem Renaissance poet, had called the Hill "the crossroads of the world."

But by the mid 1950s, the Hill was in decline. A large-scale Civic Arena project displaced thousands of residents and put many others into housing projects. Crime increased, services were lost, and residents who could afford to move did so. In 1959, Daisy Wilson married David Bedford, and the family moved from the Hill District to Hazelwood, a mostly white, working-class neighborhood. They were not welcomed — as a brick through their front window quickly revealed. Nor did Frederick August Kittel feel welcome as the only black student at the Central Catholic High School to which his mother had sent him, convinced his education would be better there than at the public school. Threats and fights became a constant part of his life. On his final day, the principal sent him home in a cab to avoid a mob of waiting students. Daisy Wilson then settled on the racially mixed Connelley Vocational High School; but the academically gifted Frederick was soon bored. He moved to Gladstone High School. But when he was in the tenth grade, a teacher accused him of plagiarizing his paper on Napoleon, implying the work was too good for a black student. He left school completely and spent his days with his books. He was a voracious reader, and his sister remembers that he would come home to share what he had learned — "He was kind of like a walking newspaper."

Frederick August Kittel moved his studies to the library, where he educated himself in the company of Langston Hughes, Richard Wright, Ralph Ellison. Despite the fact that he had learned to read when he was four, this was his first immersion in African-American literary voices. Now he knew he wanted to be a writer. But Frederick's mother wanted him to be a lawyer, and her rigorous expectations for her children led her to lovingly send her son away from her home to teach him to fend for himself. Without funds to support himself, he enlisted in the army but served only the first year of his three-year assignment. He returned to Pittsburgh.

With little official education, Frederick Kittel worked as a gardener, porter, sheet metal worker, and short-order cook in a coffee shop. He hung around on street corners and at a cigar store called Pat's Place. He was unintentionally studying the characters who would later people his plays, and as he remembers, learning how to be a man. Looking back, the writer considered this the second phase of his education, as young Kittel studied their philosophy, ideas, and attitudes. He was particularly drawn to the older men — the ones who had lived fifty or sixty years; at this time he wasn't sure he'd make it another year.

Living alone, Frederick Kittel found company in music and began collecting 78 rpm records that he bought for a nickel apiece. He collected Walter Huston, Patti Page, and Hoagy Carmichael. Then, one day while he was out searching for something new, in an old pile of records in a dime store, he found and purchased the Bessie Smith record "Nobody in Town Can Bake a Sweet Jelly Roll Like Mine." It was 1965. He put the record on his turntable and played it twenty-two times. Sometimes, years later, he'd still sing those words, "Daddy, I want some diamond rings. If you don't, I know who will."

The music played through the walls of the boarding house in which Frederick Kittel lived. It reached the array of people who stayed there, including the resident who had encouraged the careerless youth to pursue a life in counterfeiting. Kittel hadn't cared much about these people before, but Bessie Smith enabled him to understand their struggles. The music changed the way he looked at those around him, and this inspired him to write about their lives.

At age twenty, Frederick Kittell became a professional writer when his sister paid him twenty dollars to write a term paper comparing Robert Frost and Carl Sandburg. He bought a typewriter with the money, a used, thirty-five-pound Royal manual. It was a pivotal moment for the young man — his declaration that he was not going to be the lawyer his mother expected, nor was he going to be a cook or a porter. He was going to be a writer.

"The first thing I wanted to type was my name," he remembers; when he did, Freddy Kittell became August Wilson. Consciously discarding his father's history for the lineage of the mother who raised him, the young writer reviewed the paper. "I saw it and said, 'That's all right, man that's all right.' Then I began to type my poems" (unpublished 1994 interview with Joan Herrington).

His desire to write was great — so great that it sometimes hindered his other obligations. Wilson had been hanging out, writing his poems, in a booth at Eddie's diner. Knowing he needed work, the owner offered him a job and Wilson accepted. But everytime the owner looked out of the kitchen, Wilson was still sitting in the booth and writing. So Eddie fired him.

Wilson worked a series of odd jobs to pay the rent and focused on his poetry. By this time, he had read a range of poets from Amiri Baraka to John Berryman to Derek Walcott. With a few friends, Wilson started the Centre Avenue Poets Theater Workshop, which sponsored readings and published small poetry magazines. Wilson's own poetry appeared in two more-established magazines, *Black World* and *Black Lines*. He shared it whenever he could, inspiring those around him. Ben Brantley of *The New York Times*, who later visited Pittsburgh with Wilson, remembers a man who approached Wilson on the street and spoke, "When I was a windy boy and a bit, and the black spit of the chapel fold . . ." Wilson continued where the man had stopped, repeating lines from Dylan Thomas's "Lament," a poem he used to recite when he walked the streets of the Hill District.

In the late 1960s, Wilson's life began to change. In 1969, he married Brenda Burton, a black Muslim. In 1970, Sakina Ansari Wilson was born. Two years later, Wilson and Burton divorced, a result of political and religious differences. At this time, Wilson's increasing interest in politics led him to the theater. With playwright and friend Rob Penny, he founded Black Horizon on the Hill, an African-American activist theater company. Here Wilson produced and directed the plays of Ed Bullins and other African-American writers, and eventually he tried his own hand at playwriting.

Wilson had studied playwriting by studying people. He considered himself an amateur anthropologist. He watched people wherever they gathered and even remembers visiting random funeral homes — until the daughter of one of the deceased asked if he had known her father. Wilson had taken no classes and had read no books on playwriting when he tried his hand at dramatic writing. In fact, he had read very few plays — except *The Merchant of Venice* while in school. It was a purposeful choice to avoid reading plays. Wilson had read every piece of poetry he could get his hands on before he wrote in that genre, and he felt very strongly that he wanted to write his plays with a freer hand.

His first efforts were one-act plays, including *Recycle*, *The Janitor*, *The Homecoming*, and *The Coldest Day of the Year*. Although today his extraordinary dialogue inspires his audiences to participate in the drama, murmuring, "That's right" or "Tell it" during his plays, he noted (in an unpublished 1994 interview with Joan Herrington) that he was dissatisfied with these earlier efforts:

> The dialogue wasn't good. I couldn't write plays because I couldn't write dialogue. I asked [Rob Penny], "How do you make them talk," and he said "You don't make them talk — you listen to them." And I realized my mistake. I was trying to force words into their mouths instead of listening, and not

only listening but recognizing the poetry that was inherent in the way Black people spoke."

Wilson's first produced play, a musical satire entitled *Black Bart and the Sacred Hills*, the story of a stagecoach robber in the Old West, began as a long poem. At the encouragement of his friend and theater director Claude Purdy, Wilson rewrote the piece, adding six songs. Following a staged reading in Los Angeles in 1977, Purdy produced the play at the Penumbra, an African-American theater in St. Paul, Minnesota.

Wilson preferred St. Paul to his native Pittsburgh and moved there. He married Judith Oliver, Purdy's wife's best friend, who was white, and he took a job writing scripts for the Science Museum of Minnesota. He wrote short theatrical pieces such as "How the Coyote Got His Name," whose reading accompanied the diorama exhibits.

During the long cold winters, he committed himself more fully to his writing. The challenge of listening to those black voices (Wilson had transitioned from a *neighborhood* of 55,000 African Americans to a *state* with only 34,000 African Americans) forced Wilson to actively pursue his research. It also encouraged him to write his first full-length play originally conceived for the stage — *Jitney*.

Unless you call out, who will open the door?

Jitney, set in a gypsy cab station in Pittsburgh in 1971, was first produced at the Allegheny Repertory Theater in Pittsburgh in 1982. The play, Wilson's first to use realistic dialogue and to introduce the complex interweaving of characters that is now a signature of his work, was a tremendous success. Wilson was particularly encouraged by the significant number of African Americans attending the theater for the first time. He returned to St. Paul re-ignited. He joined the Playwrights' Center, and he was awarded a fellowship with a $200 per week stipend that enabled him to define himself as a professional playwright. He quit the science museum to have more time to write. Half the day he cooked for a social service organization, The Little Brothers of the

Poor; the other half of the day, he wrote. He soon began his next play, *Fullerton Street*, reflecting the clash between rural Southern and urban Northern values in the early 1940s. In this time, over 1 million African Americans had come north seeking employment and education, and the African-American community was divided. Wilson was energized by these early efforts and was eager for input. Local staged readings and workshops helped him to develop his craft.

Then in an effort to expand his regional horizons, Wilson submitted both *Jitney* and *Fullerton Street* to the Eugene O'Neill Theater Center's National Playwrights Conference in Waterford, Connecticut, in 1978 and 1980 respectively. Both were rejected, and Wilson was suitably discouraged. In 1981, Wilson summoned up his courage to once again submit a play to the O'Neill, and he mailed in his new script, *Ma Rainey's Black Bottom*. This explosive drama, centering on the legendary blues singer Ma Rainey and the musicians in her band, examines the depth of exploitation and the consequences of the tolerance of injustice.

FIRST REWARDS

In the spring of 1982, he received a telegram informing him that *Ma Rainey's Black Bottom* had been accepted for the 1982 summer conference, and Wilson's career was launched on a national scale. The following spring, Lloyd Richards, then the Artistic Director of the Conference as well as the Artistic Director of the Yale Repertory Theatre, in New Haven, Connecticut, scheduled *Ma Rainey's Black Bottom* for production at the Yale Repertory Theatre. In October 1984, the play opened on Broadway. Mr. Wilson borrowed a tuxedo; with the reviews not yet out, Wilson was unsure that he would ever need to wear it again. But *Ma Rainey* ran for 275 performances on Broadway. Even before it opened, Wilson's next play, *Fences*, was nearly complete. In fact, fearful of being a one-play playwright, Wilson had started *Fences* on the bus heading home from the O'Neill Conference.

Fences, set in the 1950s, focuses on Troy Maxson, a disenfranchised former baseball player whose career ended before African-American men were allowed to play professional baseball outside of the Negro Leagues. Troy's disappointments and his efforts to prove his manhood ultimately cause the disintegration of his family. Wilson found a model for this character in his stepfather, David Bedford, and Troy's story bears resemblance to Bedford's life. Following a disappointment in sports, a serious brush with crime brought Bedford lessons of responsibility and a more conventional post-prison life. Bedford had been a football star in high school and had hoped that a football scholarship would lead to a career in medicine. No scholarship was offered. So he robbed a store to get money to go to school. He killed a man and spent twenty-three years in prison. When he came out, Bedford met Wilson's mother and began working in the city sewer department. Bedford died in 1969 when Wilson was twenty-four.

Fences is not autobiographical. But Wilson's life does provide a cultural context in which he explores themes close to his heart. In a 1994 interview, he noted, "White America pays no attention to the Troy Maxsons in this world. They see niggers as lazy and shiftless. Well, Troy is a man who is trying to fulfill tremendous responsibility" (unpublished 1994 interview with Joan Herrington).

In July 1983, *Fences* was developed at the O'Neill Playwrights Conference. In April of 1985, *Fences* opened at the Yale Repertory Theatre, again under the direction of Lloyd Richards. Richards was a key figure in Wilson's early professional years. He credited himself with enabling Wilson to bring his work to fruition — or, at the very least, teaching him that if a character needs to change costume, then she cannot be in two contiguous scenes.

Following its run in New Haven, the production of *Fences* moved to Chicago, Seattle, and San Francisco. In March of 1987 it opened on Broadway, winning for Wilson the New York Drama Critics Circle Award for Best Play, four Antoinette Perry "Tony" Awards, and the Pulitzer Prize for Drama.

Fences was still playing on Broadway when Wilson's next play, *Joe Turner's Come and Gone*, opened one year later. It came about as a result of Wilson's thumbing through a *National Geographic* magazine. He came upon a painting by Romare Bearden entitled *Mill Hand's Lunch Bucket*. This image captivated Wilson. He was drawn to the man at the center of the image, a dark and haunting figure.

At the time Wilson discovered the painting, he was writing a poem about a newly freed slave trying to reunite with his family. By combining the story line of his poem with the image of the mysterious figure in Bearden's painting, Wilson created Herald Loomis and began a play in which he was the central character. He also found Loomis's history in an old blues song, "Joe Turner's Come and Gone," which bemoaned the fate of young African-American men who were captured at the turn of the century by Joe Turney, brother of the governor of Tennessee. Turney lured the men into gambling, and then, for their illegal activity, forced them into peonage on his plantation. Herald Loomis became a man who was separated from his wife because of his involuntary servitude to the infamous "Joe Turner."

Wilson originally titled his play *Mill Hand's Lunch Bucket*, after the painting. But he set his play in 1911, a decade before the time the painting depicts, in order to incorporate the real-life figure of Joe Turney. Wilson also wanted his play to have greater proximity to the Emancipation period, as the play centers on the search for identity. Set in Pittsburgh in 1911, *Joe Turner's Come and Gone* addresses the loss and spiritual confusion experienced by African Americans in the post-Emancipation period, a time when neither freedom nor slavery was guaranteed. This play contained a core Wilson philosophy that underlies much of his writing.

When black Americans emigrated from the South to the North they lost certain connections — connections I think we, as black Americans, need to go back and make. For 200 years we developed a culture in the south and when we moved north we abandoned that and lost our tie to our history. Kids today do not know who they are because they have no connection to their grandparents and no connection with their political history in America. (Unpublished 1994 interview with Joan Herrington)

Reconciliation of the issues of slavery also permeates Wilson's next play. In *The Piano Lesson*, set in the 1930s, Boy Willie and his sister Berniece grapple over a piano that has been carved with family images by their enslaved ancestors. At issue is the sale or maintenance of the heirloom and ultimately the denial or acceptance of the past. *The Piano Lesson* followed the same route as Wilson's other works, arriving on Broadway in April of 1990 and winning Wilson a second Pulitzer Prize for Drama. In the course of a decade, August Wilson had grown from a struggling playwright to a consistent and influential voice in the American theater. He had transitioned from the eager student of his mentor Lloyd Richards into a confident writer whose legal contracts ensured that producers did not attempt to influence the dramaturgy. By the time *Piano Lesson* arrived on the stage, Wilson was clear in his intent to write a play for each decade of the twentieth century

CONTINUED SUCCESS

As *The Piano Lesson* was opening on Broadway, *Two Trains Running* was opening at the Yale Repertory Theatre. In *Two Trains Running*, set in 1969, characters congregate in a local diner that is facing demolition in the name of urban renewal. It was a time when the destruction of small businesses and the displacement of residents was the result of city-initiated development projects. Outside the diner, rallies rage at the slaying of Malcolm X; inside the characters struggle with their everyday lives, celebrating life and death, debating politics and economics, and looking for their place in the turbulent sixties. The play reveals the lethal consequence of black America standing patiently outside the door of American society, waiting to receive its fair share. Again directed by Lloyd Richards, the play opened on Broadway in 1991.

Wilson returned to music and the music industry — originally envisioning a play with seven instruments — to write *Seven Guitars*. The play is set in the backyard of a row house on the Pittsburgh Hill in the 1940s. Floyd Barton, recently sprung from the workhouse, tries to put the pieces of his life together so that he can return to Chicago to record a few more of his songs. He battles with the forces of fate and the rage of a man long denied what the world owes to him. As the characters spiral downward, defeated by an economic world that affords them no place, Barton is stabbed to death in his own yard.

Seven Guitars arrived on Broadway in 1996 and was soon followed by *King Hedley II*, a play Wilson intended as a "sequel." The character of King Hedley is the son of a character in *Seven Guitars*. Set in the 1980s, *King Hedley II* clearly reveals a world fraught with danger. As Wilson himself notes: "Look at the sets . . . we've got a torn-down building where the guy plants some seeds and then puts barbed wire around the seeds, and everyone's walking around with 9mms under their belts. It looks like a war zone — like someone dropped a bomb there. . . ." (quoted in Kendt). The play, filled with darkness and despair, is marked by the death of a recurring Wilson character whose spiritual presence has guided the characters in several of his other plays. The unnaturally old Aunt Ester, who is either onstage or mentioned in numerous other Wilson plays, has survived from the trials of slavery to the turmoil of the Civil Rights movement. She has offered strength, guidance, and renewal throughout most of the century chronicled by Wilson; but in *King Hedley II* she dies.

THE FINAL PLAYS

Secure in his place as the predominant African-American playwright, Wilson used his prominent platform to begin to comment on and shape the future of American theatre. He became an outspoken critic of a community in which he saw no place for artists of color. Recalling the ideology of some of his inspirations from the 1960s, Wilson called for unity, and he began the final pieces of his extraordinary career.

Wilson created the bookends for his cycle in the last two plays he wrote. *Gem of the Ocean*, set in 1904 with the memory of slavery still fresh, poses the question Wilson's next one hundred years of playwriting attempts to answer; Aunt Ester, appearing onstage in this play, asks, "What use do we make of our freedom?" Closest chronologically to their African heritage and perhaps farthest from it through their proximity to slavery, the characters in *Gem of the Ocean* are desperately in need of Aunt Ester's ability to reconnect them to their cultural past. *Gem of the Ocean* premiered at the Goodman Theatre in Chicago and arrived on Broadway at the Walter Kerr Theatre in 2004.

Radio Golf, Wilson's final play in the cycle and the last to be written, presents options for the future and an age-old question reframed in a most contemporary context — how does one preserve the past and simultaneously embrace the future? The chance to revitalize a neighborhood by building an apartment complex complete with a Starbucks is challenged by one man's unwillingness to sell the old house standing in the way — not surprisingly, it is the house in which Aunt Ester lived. At the center of the play is the need to reconcile new opportunities — ranging from the successful Tiger Woods to the chance for the central character, Harmond Wilks, to be Pittsburgh's first black mayor — with a respect for and a salvation of history. The opening of *Radio Golf* at the Cort Theatre in May 2007 marked Wilson's ninth play on Broadway over a span of only twenty-three years. It is an extraordinary record for any playwright, and it changed the relationship between the American theater and its playwrights of color.

In 1991, Wilson and costume designer Constanza Romero, who would become his third wife, moved to Seattle, where he lived until his death on October 3, 2005. Here, they raised their daughter, Azula Carmen Wilson, born in 1997. Wilson loved Seattle. In the beautiful old house in which he lived, Constanza inspired him to consider painting — if he tired of writing plays. Here Wilson rode the bus — having never learned to drive — always in his canvas coat and his trademark cap. He studied the people.

But mostly, the rain kept him indoors and working, pressured by himself to always have a play in progress. Sometimes it meant staying awake all night, sitting at his desk after finishing one play, waiting for the idea that would start the next one. Wilson returned often to his native Pittsburgh and the Hill District, where he enjoyed walking the streets of his old neighborhood, greeting the people about whom he wrote and listening to their voices.

Encouraged by his own success but pursued by his own artistic demons, Wilson worked continually: "All those awards, all that stuff, I take them and I hang them on my wall. But then I turn around and my typewriter's sitting there, and it doesn't know from awards. I always tell people I'm a struggling playwright. I'm struggling to get the next play down on paper" (quoted in Rothstein).

If you refuse the advice of an elder, you will walk until sunset.

Wilson notes "most of the truly important moments in our lives go by unnoticed. [But] sometimes you are privileged to recognize these moments when they occur." For Wilson, the moment when "the universe stuttered and everything fell to a new place" was the moment he played Bessie Smith's "Nobody in Town Can Bake a Sweet Jelly Roll Like Mine" on his turntable (quoted in the Preface to *Three Plays*). It was 1965, and he played it twenty-two times.

> I was stunned. By its beauty. By its honesty. And most important by the fact that it was mine. An affirmation of my presence in the world that would hold me up and give me ground to stand on. I began to look at the occupants of my [rooming] house in a different light. I saw behind the seeming despair and emptiness of their lives a force of life, and an indomitable will that linked to their historical precedents became noble in

a place where nobility wasn't supposed to exist. (Quoted in Hampton)

This awakening to the blues and its resonance in the African-American experience had a profound effect on Wilson's work. But the blues are only one of the major influences that Wilson refers to as his "four B's": the blues, the playwright Amiri Baraka, the Argentinean short-story writer Jorge Luis Borges, and the painter Romare Bearden.

THE BLUES

This music, literature, and painting opened to Wilson a world of artistic possibility and provided him with examples that incorporated social, political, and metaphysical thought into art. As Wilson put his pen to paper, his "B's" affected the style in which he wrote, provided plots, influenced many of the smallest lines of dialogue, and determined several of the largest themes.

Wilson's plays reflect the blues' acknowledgment of a shared experience and the opportunity the music provides for commiseration and celebration. As he notes, "Anything you want to know about the black experience is in the blues. The blues is The Book — it is our sacred book" (from an unpublished 1994 interview with Joan Herrington). *Ma Rainey's Black Bottom*, which is set in the twenties and concerns the trials of the legendary blues singer, is the most obvious offspring of the influence of this music. *Seven Guitars* also has a professional bluesman at its center. But song titles, lyrics, and the blues' expression of the human condition find their way into all of Wilson's work. There are musicians in almost all the plays. And in each, the characters sing the music to find solace, to affirm their lives, to share a moment, to find their place in the world. The central character in *Joe Turner's Come and Gone*, Herald Loomis, has lost his song and must regain it in order to continue on with his life. Wilson pulled his image of the bluesman from the history of the music. A descendent of the griot, an African storyteller, the bluesman's role was to voice the truths, ironies, joys, heartbreaks, and suppressed anger of the community.

AMIRI BARAKA

The blues as music, and as cultural history, were studied extensively by the playwright Amiri Baraka (né Leroi Jones), whose political activism and aggressive playwriting thrust him to the forefront of the African-American theater movement of the 1960s. Inspired by Baraka's range of styles, Wilson experimented early in his career with plays that clearly resembled Baraka's. Ultimately, Wilson's combination of realism and spiritualism moved him stylistically away from Baraka, but he continued to explore a theme central to Baraka — the ongoing conflict between revolution and assimilation.

Baraka's call was for theater that would force change. At the core of his drama is a central character who stands up violently in the face of his oppressor, squaring off against those who hold him down. Baraka's plays include a physical embodiment of oppressive white society — one who can be killed, as Baraka often advocated. Wilson's plays also aim at ennobling life through struggle. But the confrontation undertaken by Wilson's characters is more spiritual than visceral, with the offender represented in nonphysical form. In *Ma Rainey's Black Bottom*, Levee rails against a God who did not stop the rape of his mother; in *The Piano Lesson*, Boy Willie wrestles with the ghost of the man who enslaved his forefathers; in *Joe Turner's Come and Gone*, Loomis challenges Jesus Christ; and in *Fences*, Troy beckons Mr. Death. Although the rage of Wilson's characters is just as powerful as that of Baraka's, they do not remedy their immediate oppression through violent attack. Instead, each must resolve an internal battle for self-definition and individual response to oppression before facing external foes.

JORGE LUIS BORGES

As Wilson moves the struggle of his characters from a physical to a metaphysical plane, he exhibits the influence of the Argentinean essayist and short-story writer Jorge Luis Borges. In the writings of Borges, the central characters strive to understand a seemingly incomprehensible world. Borges's tales are often fantastic and, on the surface, seem to bear no resemblance to Wilson's work. But both men write of man's need to fulfill his destiny and understand his place within a historical continuum.

Borges and Wilson are more concerned with how things happen than with what actually happens. Wilson was specifically influenced by Borges's revelation of the ending of his stories in the first lines. This forces the reader to focus on the process and not the outcome. *Seven Guitars*, which begins with the funeral of the central character and then examines the final week of his life, clearly reveals Borges's influence.

Borges's nontraditional style and transcendental themes support Wilson's preference for nonlinear form — a preference exhibited in Wilson's early work and again in his most recent plays — a theatrical style that does not follow traditional Western dramatic progression toward climax and resolution. Instead, Wilson weaves and reweaves images and motifs, steeping his audience in complex characters and their relationships.

ROMARE BEARDEN

Of the four "B's," the painter Romare Bearden has had the most direct impact on Wilson's work. Wilson remembers clearly his discovery of Romare Bearden:

> My friend Claude Purdy had purchased a copy of The Prevalence of Ritual, and one night in the fall of 1977, after dinner and much talk, he laid it open on the table before me. "Look at this," he said. "Look at this." The book lay open

on the table. I looked. What for me had been so difficult, Bearden made seem so simple, so easy. It was the art of a large and generous spirit that defined not only the character of Black American life, but also its conscience. (Quoted in Schwartzman)

Wilson studied Bearden, appreciating his ability to capture the energy of an entire community in a single work of art. Following this lead, Wilson's plays do not reveal struggle within what has become the common context for contemporary drama in which the temporary problem of the individual is addressed and most often solved. Rather, Wilson and Bearden depict struggles in an African-American context — i.e., struggles that are ongoing and that reflect problems facing a community rather than an individual. Bearden's imagery encouraged Wilson to incorporate into his work elements that define traditional African performance forms. These include recognizable details of everyday life, a cycle of life including birth and death, existence influenced by past and future generations. Bearden and Wilson searched for, and found, the ritualistic roots that reward their work with timeless application.

Bearden also provided Wilson with a collection of powerful visual images — images marking the history of a people — that pervade Wilson's texts: trains, guitar players, birds, conjure women. And two Bearden collages, *Mill Hand's Lunch Bucket* and *The Piano Lesson*, directly inspired Wilson to create the drama of the characters pictured at their centers (*Mill Hand's Lunch Bucket* became *Joe Turner's Come and Gone*).

THE WRITING PROCESS

Working in the same method as Romare Bearden, his spiritual mentor, Wilson created a play through the process of collage. For months, even years, before he wrote a play, he assembled bits and pieces. Wilson thought best in busy, noisy coffee shops, moving from one to another, ordering java, and awaiting inspiration. Amid the crowd and noise, Wilson gathered bits of dialogue as interactions among characters played out in his head. He held them in his mind. Sometimes he wrote them on small scraps of paper or even napkins. Wilson saved these bits and pieces of conversation; he recited them to friends, refining them and extending them. Then he put them on a large canvas.

In the center of the canvas, Wilson may have applied an image taken, for example, from a painting — a brooding man at a table, or a girl sitting at a piano. Then he looked for connections between his bits of dialogue and his images. He may have joined his images with words from a blues song — "Joe Turner's Come and Gone" or "Two Trains Running." He may have pulled the ties from incidents in African-American history — a Martin Luther King rally, enslavement by the infamous Joe Turney, or a well-remembered title fight. The inclusions are not necessarily accurate in chronological placement or detail; it is not Wilson's intent to chronicle great and important events but rather to capture the history of a people in their struggle and their everyday lives. Influenced by his "B's," he wrote from the culture of each decade — music and literature and visual art — as opposed to historical research.

Wilson is not an autobiographical writer but elements of his life appear in the details of his plays. Names are borrowed: Zonia and Bynum in *Joe Turner's Come and Gone* are named for Wilson's grandparents; Sara Legree in *Two Trains Running* is named for a Christian missionary from Wilson's boyhood neighborhood. Characteristics are remembered and reassigned. Two Wilson characters, Troy and Levee, who cannot read, recall Wilson's uncle and an old friend, both of whom were illiterate.

Once all the pieces had been assembled, Wilson began the process of putting them into an effective dramatic structure. And this was done largely through experimentation — moving pieces of a scene around within the scene or to an entirely different part of the play, moving whole sections of a play from one act to another.

Wilson worked on his plays for several years before they ever reached full production, and he did not write in isolation. He strongly supported the play-development process and felt that an author needed an extended period of time to "discover" a play. Workshops and rehearsals provided a chance for him to see a play "on its feet" and test its rhythm. While Wilson might have pored over his computer screen for hours, his discoveries were greater when he heard his words aloud. Even in the early stages of his work, Wilson wanted actors to speak his lines, directors to stage his scenes, and audiences to tell him when they were confused. He continually sought out the company of theater artists and organizations who devoted their energies to developing new work. His plays had readings and productions at institutions dedicated to the refinement of new American drama. Wilson's plays were honed through long meetings at New Dramatists in New York, staged readings at the Eugene O'Neill Theater Center's National Playwrights Conference, a premiere at the Yale Repertory or Goodman Theatre, and a series of regional productions in which the plays underwent significant change on their way to Broadway.

A CALL TO ACTION

Wilson's deep investment in mainstream American theater came under scrutiny when, in 1996, at the annual conference of the Theatre Communications Group, held at Princeton University, he issued an urgent warning: ". . . black theatre today . . . [is] a target for cultural imperialists who seek to propagate their ideas about the world as the only valid ideas, and see blacks as woefully deficient not only in arts and letters but in the abundant gifts of humanity." Reviewing the status of black theater, Wilson challenged black artists to reconsider where, how, and for whom their plays are produced. "It is time," he said, "we took responsibility for our talents in our own hands" (quoted in "Ground on Which I Stand").

Certainly Wilson was an appropriate proponent for the contemporary black theater, but his increasing outspokenness on racial politics in the arts illuminated an incongruity between his ideology and his own artistic practice. Indeed, Wilson's very success has provided him with a platform from which he repudiated the theatrical route he himself had followed.

Wilson's speech was no doubt inspired by a then-increasing vogue in North American theaters for work by black playwrights — a trend he himself certainly strengthened by his success. Theaters that were once almost exclusively the domain of white playwrights were making a point of including the occasional work by black artists. Wilson denounced this trend as devastating to the life of black theater because it meant that white theaters were siphoning off money — and audiences — that would otherwise be available to black theaters. Offering an alternate plan for the survival and flourishing of black culture, Wilson called for the establishment of more theaters devoted to the production of black plays, and challenged black artists to support these theaters with their own work.

The speech, delivered to a predominantly white audience, sparked immediate discussion throughout the theater community. Indeed, Wilson's attacks on white theater's attempts at multiculturalism and his implicit criticism of those minority artists who participate in such efforts were unexpected, coming as they did from a black playwright whose success had been built with the support of so many white theaters.

Wilson's speech also raised questions about his own creative process. Central to Wilson's argument against diversification was the adverse effect white theaters have on black artists who "allow others to have authority over our culture and spiritual products." Wilson warned of tremendous danger in these circumstances, saying: "We are being strangled by our well-meaning friends. Money spent 'diversifying' the American theatre . . . only strengthens and solidifies this stranglehold by making our artists subject to the paternalistic notions of white institutions that dominate and control art." (Quoted in "August Wilson Responds")

As soon as Wilson's speech was published, it aroused debate in the field. Perhaps the most outspoken critic of Wilson's racial exclusiveness was Robert Brustein, founder of both the Yale Repertory and the American Repertory Theatres. In a debate in Town Hall, New York City, inspired by the controversy surrounding the Theatre Communications Group address, and moderated by Anna Deavere Smith, Brustein and Wilson exchanged views about production, funding, inclusivity, and diversity. As two of the American Theater's foremost artists and spokesmen sparred, the community was inspired to continue conversation on these complex issues.

Brustein defended the right of black theater artists to appear in plays written by whites, and he challenged Wilson to bring his own work to black theaters, raising questions of both racial politics and artistic process. Had the development of Wilson's plays at white institutions endangered his creative cultural identity? Except for the original act of creating the first draft of the play, all of Wilson's efforts are influenced by the American process of play development — a process in which new plays are open to some degree of professional and public review in the course of their creation. At institutions recognized within the professional theater as bastions for the progression of new work — and New Dramatists and the O'Neill Playwrights Conference are only two of the dozens existing — plays are staged by eager personnel, poked at by examining directors and dramaturges, molded by ambitious artistic directors, and deluged with comments from theater professionals. Wilson was committed to this process.

THE ONGOING DEBATE

Many contemporary theater artists believe that the practitioners of American dramaturgy may not truly have the playwright's integrity in mind. Some Wilson critics, or perhaps those who believe themselves his truest fans, argue that the pressures of the developmental institutions tend to produce plays written in the Western, naturalistic tradition, and moved Wilson away from his impulse to write in a nontraditional Western mode and closer to African storytelling. Robert Brustein was an outspoken voice on this point, as he wrote about Wilson's work in *The New Republic* in 1990.

> If Wilson wishes to remain a truly major playwright, he would be wise to move on from safe, popular sociology and develop the radical poetic strain that now lies dormant in his art. It is not easy to forsake the rewards of society for the rewards of posterity, but the genuine artist accepts no standards lower than the exacting ones he applies to himself.

Brustein warned Wilson against becoming the "cultural equivalent of affirmative action." He believed Wilson's work had been pushed toward the mainstream, while at the same time using the "raging polemics" of earlier African-American playwrights.

But critic and dramaturge Michael Feingold believes that Wilson's pressure comes as much from within as without.

> I think one thing you get in August is two very different aesthetics going on, and I think he has, probably, conflicted impulses about them (the way any artist does). He wants to do two quite different things at the same time. One is a sort of condition of talk, as music, that makes the plays conversation pieces that are sometimes very static and very beautiful. And the other one is an effort to do a well-crafted play in the old style. (Feingold in an unpublished 1994 interview with Joan Herrington)

Study of Wilson's plays, particularly those written after *Ma Rainey's Black Bottom*, does indicate that the development process moved Wilson away from his impulse to write in a mode that is closer to African literary and performance traditions, and more clearly reflective of the influence of his four "B's." What binds Wilson and his four "B's" together is their individual abilities to create contemporary art that is empowered by the incorporation of cultural traditions and sensibilities. This is most clearly reflected in Wilson's early drafts, which are consistent in their inclusion of extensive storytelling, nonrealistic elements, and sprawling narrative.

But by the time the plays reached Broadway, they had become much more akin to commercial Western drama. Indeed, the study of the progressive drafts of many of Wilson's scripts reveals the melding of his original artistic impulses with mainstream theatrical conventions. The conflict and resolution he underwent are perhaps the artistic equivalent of the conflict examined by the plays themselves — African Americans' continuing embrace and denial of their African past.

Whether or not his associations have in any way limited Wilson's work, the collaboration has resulted in great critical and commercial success for Wilson. It's difficult to dismiss pressure that results in tremendous audience response and two Pulitzer Prizes. In less then twenty-five years, he has had nine plays on Broadway and one off-Broadway. No contemporary playwright can compare. Wilson himself expresses no regrets. Reviewing his own work, he claimed, "I ain't sorry for nothin' I done." (Unpublished 1994 interview with Joan Herrington)

People without a sense of themselves are like a tribe wandering through the darkness without direction.

We were land-based agrarian people from Africa. We were uprooted from Africa, and we spent over 200 years developing our culture as black Americans. And then we left the South. We uprooted ourselves and attempted to transplant this culture to the pavements of the industrialized North. And it was a transplant that did not take. I think if we had stayed in the South, we would have been a stronger people. In all my plays, I always point toward making that connection, toward reconnecting with the past. You have to know who you are, and understand your history in America over more than 300 years, in order to know what your relation is to your society. (Wilson quoted in Rothstein)

Looking out over history, August Wilson bemoaned the great migration north to a place where African Americans were never equal. Between 1915 and 1930, it is estimated that 1.3 million African Americans moved from the South to the North and Midwest. In the following forty years, perhaps as many as 5 million more relocated. The resulting oppression, exploitation, and pressure to assimilate are found in all of his plays as the characters struggle to reconcile past and present. Wilson's characters face all the trappings of contemporary white-dominated society — falsely golden representatives of economic possibility, semblance of acceptance, the lure of false equality. And in a call to seek a better path, Wilson juxtaposes these temptations with traditional elements of African culture. Griots, cultural rituals, and even sacrifice weave through all the plays as characters move closer and farther from their cultural past. Disconnected, Wilson's characters are struggling to find their place in the world. Throughout this century Wilson saw African Americans whose tie to the greater community — a source of strength required for survival — had been severed; his plays examine this separation and advocate for a essential reconnection in a passionate call for self-definition.

Crucial to the African-American search for self is a move away from the dangers of assimilation and the often-resultant exploitation. Wilson exemplified the dangers as he examined the impact of the black man's adoption of white religion and his desire to find a place in professional sports and music. Throughout his plays Wilson reflects a deeply embedded inequality on which American society is built. But he does not advocate for an outright rejection of the elements of white culture that he sees as implanted in African-American life. Rather he advocates for a questioning of the value of these elements and then a balance between the new and the old — a balance in which African cultural past and African-American history have a significant place in contemporary African-American life. In "A Playwright Talks About the Blues," Wilson noted:

> I think it was Amiri Baraka who said that when you look in the mirror you should see your God. All over the world, nobody has a God who doesn't resemble them. Except black Americans. They can't even see they're worshipping someone else's God, because they want so badly to assimilate, to get the fruits of society. The message of America is "Leave your Africanness outside the door." My message is claim what is yours.

In several of his plays, Wilson's characters directly challenge the interest of the white man's god in the black man's life. In *Ma Rainey's Black Bottom*, when Cutler tells the story of the life-threatening humiliation of an African-American minister by several white men, Levee offers a blistering response: "Why didn't God strike some of them crackers down? Tell me that! . . . He a man of God . . . Why didn't god strike some of them crackers down. I'll tell you why! . . . 'Cause he's a white man's God . . . God ain't never listened to no nigger's prayers." His fire is fueled by the memory of the rape of his mother by a gang of white men carried out as she cried out to Jesus.

In *Joe Turner's Come and Gone*, the central character, Loomis, delivers a scathing indictment of Jesus Christ himself. Deacon Loomis's enslavement began when he was captured by a post-slavery plantation owner while he was spreading the gospel. After having served his seven years, Loomis meets up with his lost wife, who, in an effort to save the seemingly destroyed man, recites the Lord's Prayer. Loomis responds: "You can't tell me nothing about no valleys. I done been all across the valleys and the hills and the mountains and the oceans . . . And all I seen was a bunch of niggers dazed out of their wooly heads. And Mr. Jesus Christ standing there in the middle of them grinning. . . . He grin that big old grin . . . and them niggers wallowing at his feet."

In Wilson's plays, the imbalance of power, bred by subservience to a white man's god, is only one manifestation of the imbalance of power between black men and white men — even white men who seem interested in offering help. Thus, Wilson creates characters who ostensibly provide opportunity — advance careers, sell their wares — but he does so with painful irony.

In *Joe Turner's Come and Gone*, Selig, the "people finder" who offers to help Loomis find his wife, proudly describes his history: " . . . we been finders in my family for a long time. Bringers and finders. My great-granddaddy used to bring nigras across the ocean on ships. That wasn't no easy job either . . . Me and my daddy have found plenty of nigras. My daddy, rest his soul, used to find runaway slaves for plantation bosses . . . Had him a reputation stretched clean across the country."

Ma Rainey's manager, Irvin, is described by Wilson as "a man who prides himself on his knowledge of African Americans and his ability to deal with them." He cannot, however, remember any of the names of the musicians in Ma's band. He, like other white men who offer false promise to the black man, represents a warning by Wilson against dependence on those who profess sympathy but whose actions reveal ignorance or benign neglect, at best.

THE BATTLE FOR JUSTICE

A societally ingrained lack of opportunity and lack of equality is evidenced throughout the Wilson canon. *King Hedley II*, set in the decaying, violent Hill District of Pittsburgh in 1985, examines the title character's striving to start a new life following a seven-year jail term for manslaughter. King's journey begins with Wilson's stark presentation of the reality of a life in which unseparate and unequal plagues the characters. King's inability to have even his most modest expectations met is evidenced in his speech following his unsuccessful visit to a Sears store to pick up his photos. Despite the fact that he brings his receipt, as instructed, he is unable to fulfill even this simple quest: "The problem is they tell me my receipt don't count. That's what the problem is . . . You see what I'm saying. That's like telling me I don't count."

Indeed, at every turn King is told he does not count and quickly comes to recognize the basic injustice of his world. "They got everything stacked up against you as it is. Every time I try to do something they get in the way. It's been that way my whole life. Every time I try to do something they get in the way." Raised at the height of the Civil Rights movement, King and his wife, Tonya, expected better but now recognize that impossibility. Tonya rues her children's future: "Wasn't nothing for me and now ain't nothing for them . . . Seem like something should have changed."

Hambone in *Two Trains Running* has struggled and lost the battle with justice. Promised a ham in exchange for work done for a white man, Hambone has never recovered from the reneging of this promise. Troy Maxson, the father at the center of *Fences*, fought to use his talent for baseball to earn his living and was pushed back by the white establishment, which had no place for black athletes. The scars he bears from this disappointment have marked his life as his need to establish his own self-worth eventually causes the destruction of his family. In his pursuit of a more stable life for his son, Cory, Troy denies him the one thing he desires most — the opportunity to play college football — and Cory leaves his father's home. And in the drive to feel more alive, Troy has an affair and brings home the other woman's child to his wife, following his mistress's death in childbirth.

Troy and other men in Wilson's canon make the choices they feel they must make when faced with ongoing oppression. They struggle and do what they feel they need to do to survive. King Hedley dreams of opening a video store — in fact one video store in each state. Without other opportunity, he finances his entrepreneurial dreams by selling refrigerators of questionable origin and by robbing the local jewelry store. He, like other Wilson characters, feeds his family — and his sense of justice — through illegal activity. Wilson does not judge these men negatively but rather sees them as warriors. He noted in conversation with Bill Moyers that he respected those "who look around to see what the society has cut out for them, who see the limits of their participation, and are willing to say, 'No I refuse to accept this limitation that you are imposing on me . . .'"

Throughout Wilson's plays there are men who take what they are owed or offer what is due. In *Gem of the Ocean*, Solly, a past conductor of the Underground Railroad, burns down the mill whose owners abuse their workers. Sterling, *Two Trains Running's* growing black nationalist, steals the ham that was owed to the character Hambone, who was never adequately paid for work done.

While Wilson's respect for the valiance of these undertakings is clear, they are not separable from other, less valiant actions. Wilson's concern is expressed by the women of his plays who recognize the inherent challenge to the structure of the community and its families posed by these choices. In *Two Trains Running*, Risa tells the proposing Sterling, "You ain't got no job. You going back to the penitentiary. I don't want to be tied up with nobody I got to be worrying is they gonna rob another bank or something." In *King Hedley II*, King's wife Tonya tells his mother, Ruby: "Every time he go out somewhere I hold my breath. I'm tired of it. I'm suffocating myself. I done told him if he go back to jail I'm through with it. I gonna pack up my little stuff and leave. I ain't goin' through that again. I ain't visiting any more jailhouses." In Wolfe's *August Wilson*, Carla McDonough notes that society has taught these men to "prize masculinity over community in the forms of family, home, neighborhood." And while Wilson respects the necessity of the choice these men make, he recognizes, nonetheless, the need to change the culture that breeds these choices.

For some, misguided pursuits, combined with no tether to the core of the community, create a world of frustration and disappointment. Stifled by the roadblocks society has laid down, these characters vent their rage on each other, resulting in the disintegration of families and the black-on-black violence that came to exemplify urban life throughout the twentieth century.

In *Ma Rainey's Black Bottom* the action centers on a recording session by Ma Rainey and her band in a Chicago studio. All day, the characters wait to lay down their music. Ultimately, the record is cut, but the exploitative conditions lead to a violent confrontation. Levee, the newest member has seen the destruction caused by racial oppression but now he turns a blind eye knowing that the prize he covets — the opportunity to write and record his songs with his own band — can only be awarded by the white man. Here and in play after play, Wilson reveals the specious pursuit of the unattainable prize as intensely destructive.

Wilson purposefully set this play within the world of the blues where Levee, like many other Wilson characters, reveals his distance from his heritage. Levee's consistent rejection of traditional blues is a denial of a cultural connection — a denial he makes in an effort at assimilation — a denial that is ultimately self-destructive. Ma tries to explain to Levee the significance of the music beyond the notes: "Folks don't understand about the blues. They hear it come out but they don't understand how it got there. They don't understand that's life's way of talking. You don't sing to feel better. You sing cause that's a way of understanding life."

Levee does not recognize the value of the old ways nor does he acknowledge the reality of Ma's relationship to the music industry despite her clear warning:

> They don't care nothing about me. All they want is my voice. Well, I done learned that, and they gonna treat me like I want to be treated no matter how much it hurt them . . . As soon as they get my voice down on them recording machines,

then it's just like if I'd be some whore and they roll over and put their pants on. Ain't got no use for me then.

Levee believes he can beat the system: "As soon as I get my band together and make them records like Mr. Sturdyvant done told me I can make, I'm gonna be like Ma and tell the white man just what he can do . . . That's the way I'm gonna be! Make the white man respect me." Levee plays by the white man's rules and he loses. Ultimately, he realizes that he has accepted a society that refuses to recognize his worth or allow him to contribute. His existence denied, Levee explodes and Wilson exposes the self-destructive nature of the Levee's tolerance of racism. With no other outlet for his anger, Levee stabs and kills his fellow band member, Toledo, for stepping on his shoe.

The moment is a tragedy repeated in other Wilson plays. But in the darkness, Wilson sees the potential for rebirth in the redefinition of self. At the beginning of *Joe Turner's Come and Gone*, Herald Loomis arrives in Pittsburgh with his daughter, Zonia. For three years, they have been searching for Loomis's wife. Loomis was separated from his wife because of his involuntary servitude to the infamous "Joe Turner." Turner was immortalized in the blues song, "Joe Turner's Come and Gone," which bemoaned the fate of young African-American men who were captured at the turn of the century by Joe Turney, brother of the governor of Tennessee. Turney (who an old blues song made "Turner") lured the men into gambling, and then, for their illegal activity, forced them into peonage on his plantation.

Wilson makes clear that Loomis's bondage did not end with the termination of his physical enslavement. Having lost his identity, Loomis is an empty man when he enters the boardinghouse where the play is set. Ultimately, the faith and magic of Bynum, a modern-day conjure man, enables Loomis to accept his past and use the strength of his culture to move forward. He becomes self-sufficient, "resurrected, cleansed," and free.

CONNECTING TO THE PAST

As with all Wilson plays, *Joe Turner's Come and Gone* is a call to reestablish the cultural connection, i.e., the recognition of the link between personal and cultural history, and the incorporation of cultural traditions into contemporary lives. It was the first Wilson play to examine the relationship of African mysticism to the contemporary lives of his characters and the potential for what Wilson terms "African retentions" that serve as both a source of strength and a kind of psychic balm for twentieth-century African Americans.

At the end of Act I, Loomis finds the other characters in the kitchen, doing a Juba dance and invoking the Holy Ghost. The Juba dance originated in West Africa and existed on the plantations. Its stomping, clapping, and other sounds were a way to facilitate otherwise forbidden communication. Here, as in other places in his plays Wilson places Christian and African culture side by side in an effort to encourage the embrace of the later even in conjunction with the former. Bertha, the boardinghouse owner and a church-going woman, still lines coins up on her windowsill to keep evil out.

But Loomis, a former preacher struggling with the inconstancies of his faith and his history, condemns the action in the kitchen and then is overtaken by a haunting vision of bones walking on the water. Loomis then sees the bones sink back into the water and rise up as fully formed men who look like him; he is terrified.

> I done seen bones rise up out of the water. Rise up and walk across the water. Bones walking on top of the water. Come to this place . . . to this water that was bigger than the whole world. And I looked out . . . and I seen theses bones rise up out the water. Rise up and begin to walk on top of it . . They just walking across the water . . . and then . . . they sunk down . . . when they sink down they made a big splash and this here wave come up . . . It washed them out of the water

and upon the land. Only . . . only . . . They got flesh on them . . . Just like you and me!

In his vision, Loomis tries to walk with the bones people but cannot because he refuses to recognize his connection to them; he refuses to acknowledge that he has been deeply affected by his bondage. But Loomis's vision of the bones people, a metaphoric representation of those who died during the Middle Passage and early slavery, and who are now rising to take their place in the world ultimately forces him to recognize his place in the world. With coaching from Bynum, Loomis acknowledges that those rising up are are ". . . Black. Just like you and me," and he comes to understand that he must join them in order to be whole.

Wilson returns again and again to his clear mandate to reconnect to the past and to find personal strength therein. In *The Piano Lesson*, Berniece is emotionally crippled, filled with rage and hate; she cannot begin to approach the heirloom piano, alive with the spirits of her enslaved ancestors whose images have been carved into the instrument's legs. But at the end of the play, when her brother Boy Willie is battling the ghost of the landowner who enslaved their forefathers, Berniece sits at the piano and Wilson describes the moment in his stage direction: "She begins to play. The song is found piece by piece. It is an old urge to song that is both a commandment and a plea. With each repetition it gains strength. It is intended as an exorcism and a dressing for battle. A rustle of wind blowing across the continents." In *Gem of the Ocean*, the City of Bones returns. In this play, Aunt Ester attends Citizen Barlow who is troubled by having committed a robbery for which an innocent man has chosen to give his life rather than be branded a thief. In order to make him "whole," Aunt Ester takes Barlow on a journey to the City of Bones, re-creating the experience of the Middle Passage and enabling him to find peace through acknowledgment of that history.

MEMORY OF THE ANCESTORS

Aunt Ester made her first "entrance" in *Two Trains Running* in which the character Holloway notes: "Aunt Ester give you more than money. She make you right with yourself." Unseen but present in this play and the three that follow, Aunt Ester is defined by her actions and words related by those onstage. For Wilson's characters, she holds the potential for spiritual renewal through connection to the past. She preaches self-knowledge and personal responsibility. As Holloway tells Sterling, "You don't want to do nothing for yourself. You want somebody else to do it for you. Aunt Ester don't work that way. he say you got to pull your part of the load."

For Ester, and Wilson, pulling the load means acknowledging where you have come from. In *Two Trains Running*, Memphis comments, "Aunt Ester clued me on this one. I went up there and told her my whole life story. She says, "If you drop the ball, you got to go back and pick it up. Ain't no need in keeping running, cause if you get to the end zone it ain't gonna be a touchdown." Aunt Ester stands as Wilson's ever-present reminder of the need for connection to the past. For his characters, she is the conduit to the source. Ester makes her debut stage appearance in *Gem of the Ocean*, chronologically Wilson's first play, set in 1904. In *King Hedley II*, she dies.

Born in 1619 and, at the opening of *King Hedley II*, three hundred and sixty-six years old, Aunt Ester's life has spanned the presence of the African people on Western soil. Despite the fact that she only makes an appearance in one play, *Gem of the Ocean*, Wilson notes in the preface to *King Hedley II*:

> Aunt Ester has emerged for me as the most significant persona of the cycle. The characters, after all, are her children. The wisdom and tradition she embodies are valuable tools for the reconstruction of their personalities and for dealing with a society in which the contradictions, over the decades, have grown more fierce, and for exposing all the places it is

lacking in virtue . . . Aunt Ester carries the memory of all Africans, the memory of the ancestors. She embodies the wisdom and traditions of all those Africans, starting with the first one. It is a tremendous responsibility to carry all this — to remember for everyone as well as to remember for yourself — and she's accepted the responsibilities of it.

The "death" of Aunt Ester, and the demands this event makes on Wilson's characters stand as the metaphysical core of *King Hedley II* and, indeed, of all Wilson's plays. Her deep presence in this play, ironically in spite of her physical absence, calls to the fore African culture and forces its integration into a world where it does not exist in sufficient force to empower Ester's survival. Perhaps, the characters conjecture, Aunt Ester died of grief, certainly a possibility as she surveyed a landscape in which she had no place. As the character Stool Pigeon describes, "The people wandering all over the place. They got lost. They don't even know the story of how they got from tit to tat. Aunt Ester know but the path to her house is all grown over with weeds, can't hardly find the door no more."

Aunt Ester's impossible old age calls into question her existence in a world defined by twentieth-century Western culture, deeply dependent on linear chronological progression and clear lines between life and death. Throughout Wilson's century-long saga, his characters consistently note that Aunt Ester is unnaturally old, unnaturally wise, and indeed, otherworldly. But viewed from the African, particularly Yoruban context, her presence is less unusual. Called forth and made present by their descendents, ancestors exist within the same world as those who follow them. They exist in the here and now, and one encounters them at the crossroads of life or invokes them in moments of crisis. It is an idea Wilson invoked in *The Piano Lesson* as Berniece called to her ancestors to aid in her brother's struggle.

In *King Hedley II*, Stool Pigeon buries Aunt Ester's black cat in the backyard. Given societal restrictions, it is the closest he can come to burying Aunt Ester herself at the site of the house in keeping with a tradition wherein ancestors were kept close to home. Despite objections by those in the house, Stool Pigeon creates the grave in preparation for his anticipated spilling of blood onto the site so that the cat (representative of Aunt Ester) can come back in seven days. The ritual sacrifice is not needed so much to resurrect Aunt Ester as to resurrect the community through a reconnection to its spiritual and cultural past.

Whether she lives on the earth in a mortal state or whether her "death" is merely the symbolic identification of the severing of the ties to her "children," whose acknowledgment of her existences is necessary for her sustenance, her neglect and her death is the core of all Wilson tragedy. As Molefi Kete Asante notes in "The Future of African Gods: The Class of Civilizations," "the abandonment of our history, indeed the abandonment of our gods, the gods of our ancestors, have brought us deep into the quagmire of misdirection, misorientation and self pity — a quagmire demanding a sacrifice."

In his call for a vital reconnection, particularly in the later plays, Wilson himself clearly re-engages with African culture connecting again and again with traditional demand for ritual and sacrifice as a means of achieving harmony. In *Joe Turner's Come and Gone*, Bynum sacrifices a rooster in a ritual dance; in *Seven Guitars*, Hedley also sacrifices a rooster. It is an act shocking to those both in the audience and those on the stage, intended to startle them into recognition of the danger of their complacent acceptance of inequality.

THE POWER OF SACRIFICE

Wilson recognizes that it requires a lasting ritual to return the community to a state of balance. In *King Hedley II*, when Stool Pigeon buries Aunt Ester's cat, he knows that blood on the grave of this animal will ensure its return in seven days — and he seeks an appropriate animal to sacrifice. But Wilson returned to one of the most powerful and drastic moments in a community's attempt at regeneration; Wilson recognized the need for the sacrifice of a king.

The play concludes with the accidental shooting of the title character by his mother. It is a heart-stopping moment, seemingly epitomizing the agonizing cycle of violence that defines this generation. It seems at first akin to the senseless deaths of Toledo in *Ma Rainey* and Floyd Barton in *Seven Guitars*. But in *King Hedley II*, Wilson has framed it differently. Immediately following King's shooting, the stage directions read, "Stool Pigeon suddenly recognizes that the sacrifice has been made." King's blood has fallen on the grave of the black cat belonging to Aunt Ester. It is the sacrifice that Stool Pigeon has been awaiting, one that will enable the resurrection of Aunt Ester and reconnection of the community to a lost past. For Wilson and for us, it is a moment of transition — of hope.

Here, perhaps, Wilson is reading the patterns in the divining tray, using a Yoruban tradition to determine the appropriate road toward healing on which to send his characters. He, like Aunt Ester, is a truth sayer. As such, she is part of a collection of "seers" scattered throughout Wilson's work, for Wilson does not allow his characters to travel this difficult journey toward reconciliation unattended. They are guided by a collection of soothsayers who see a light leading out of an oppressive time. Ironically, they are frequently characters viewed by their peers and the audience as being less grounded in reality than others on the stage. Each has been wounded, exploited, and damaged through denial of what they have earned. In response to their internalized oppression, Gabe, Troy Maxson's brother in *Fences*, Hambone in *Two Trains Running*, Hedley in *Seven Guitars*, and Stool Pigeon in *King Hedley II* all envision a greater place for themselves — be it alongside St. Peter, or as a crowned king — and a possibility for a bright "afterlife" that follows the dark present. In their demands for what is due to them or their railings against the status quo, their truth is a call to action and the pursuit of a road toward salvation for the community. They look to the future — to a time of greater peace within the community, a time of willingness to embrace the past. It will be a time of jubilation — an end to all enslavement, and it is an old idea in African-American culture.

In *Past as Present in the Drama of August Wilson*, Harry Elam notes that "During slavery times, the notion of jubilee, a Judgment Day when the terrors of slavery would be overcome, offered slaves hope in something after slavery, an afterlife, salvation." In Wilson's plays, it is most specifically Gabe, Aunt Ester, and Stool Pigeon who look toward the judgment day as Wilson uses these characters as a final reminder of the relationship between the beginning and the end, a cycle of life ever present in African culture. And again Wilson blends elements of past and present. In a traditional Christian sense, throughout *Fences*, Gabe speaks of Saint Peter and the names in his book. But when Troy dies and Gabe goes to blow his horn that he carries always in the ready to open the gates, his trumpet makes no sound. At this moment he must look elsewhere — behind and deep within. Wilson describes the moment: "He begins to dance. A slow, strange dance, eerie and life giving. A dance of atavistic signature and ritual. . . . He finishes the dance and the gates of heaven stand open as wide as God's closet." In *Gem of the Ocean*, Solly has learned through Aunt Ester about the City of Bones and he says, "It's a beautiful city. That's where I'm going when I die. I know where I'm going. Got Twelve Gates and it's got Twelve Gatekeepers." In a blending of cultures, the Gatekeeper writes down names and like Peter, he can deny entry. But inside are people who look like Solly and all the other characters in Wilson's plays, and they are glorious.

At the conclusion of *King Hedley II*, when Stool Pigeon prepares the heavens to receive King he calls to "the conquering Lion of Judea," a reference to the King characters from this play and *Seven Guitars*, black men who were redeemers of their community. What is key, as Harry Elam note, is that "Stool Pigeon is calling out a God who looks like him, who understands the history of black struggle and survival and who can and will response to black needs." He has fused the disparate parts and he is claiming, for the entire community, what Wilson believes is rightfully theirs.

For tomorrow belongs to the people who prepare for it today.

Over thirty-five years of writing plays, August Wilson's friends and associates witnessed his blossoming as an artist, his growing security in his craft, and his ever-increasing pleasure with working in the theater. Wilson's process of writing remained essentially the same. For years before he set pen to paper, he lived with people he did not know, men and women who filled his imagination with the stories of their lives. Sometimes Wilson had already heard what they came to tell him; sometimes, they surprised him with their history or their humor. Emerging characters sat with Wilson in coffee shops, followed him on the street, and accompanied him on airplanes. And he listened to their every word.

> I believe that whatever a character says is true. So I write down everything the character says — pages and pages. Then, the trick is weeding through all that and finding the story that is really buried in there. And sometimes you really have to dig. You have to discover the connection of all the characters to the story that you're writing, to the play. That's the fun part. (1994 unpublished interview with with Joan Herrington)

Wilson recorded the individual tales and then he searched for common threads. Sometimes he bound his characters and their stories with the words to a song he remembered; sometimes he drew them into an image from a painting he had admired. New lives began to appear on pieces of paper as Wilson pursued James Baldwin's call for "a profound articulation of the Black tradition" — for Wilson "that field of manners and ritual of intercourse that will sustain a man once he's left his father's house." (1994 unpublished interview with Joan Herrington)

Wilson was never without a play in his head. Joe Adcock reports that director Dan Sullivan witnessed the glorious immersion: "The last time I saw him . . . he was standing on the corner of 47th Street and

Broadway [in Manhattan] right in the middle of the sidewalk. I was going to say hello, as I normally would. But something told me, no, he's concentrating. He was smiling. His eyes were full of ideas. I said to myself: 'Don't interrupt. He's writing.'"

Wilson is remembered by his compatriots as open-minded and continually rewriting, even in performance where he carefully watched the theater patrons night after night. Wilson's process of playwriting produces plays lauded by artists, audiences, and critics. Testament to the magnitude and honesty of Wilson's characters are the responses of actors and actresses who have performed in Wilson's plays. For Charles Dutton, a Wilson play is anything but work:

> In an August Wilson play, for an actor, you basically, for two and a half to three hours, you basically can leave this life. In doing one of his plays you can get so engrossed and wrapped up in his works that you can, for the time that you're doing that play, you can leave this life. And it is a joy ride. A glorious, theatrical joyride that you get few and far between. (Unpublished interview with Joan Herrington, 1993)

Roscoe Lee Brown, who performed in *Joe Turner's Come and Gone*, lights up when he discusses Wilson's plays.

> Isn't it extraordinary writing? Having had the real good fortune to work in the theater with great poets and dramatists, I put August Wilson very high in that pantheon. I believe absolutely that he is every bit as good as O'Neill. He plumbs the psyche as surely as any of the great dramatists and he knows how to summon up race memories that make you whole. (Quoted in Tallmer)

Wilson has succeeded in creating powerful dramas recognizable to all who encounter them. His plays are a vital encapsulation of African-American history and contemporary life. They are chronicles of men and women whose constant upheaval has left them searching.

They are quests for historical and spiritual truths among a people who have been continually uprooted. Wilson's plays are very specific to the African-American experience. Yet, his work has great relevance to all artists and audiences.

Wilson's final two plays were the first and last in the cycle. Although this was not an intentional choice, in doing so, Wilson created a circle. It is a continuum in which all life — ancestral, the living, and the unborn — simultaneously exist. And at the center of this world, as Aunt Ester notes in *Gem of the Ocean*, is the City of Bones. It is the core from which all strength is drawn. Its energy radiates throughout the community. August Wilson has revealed to us the glory of its embrace.

DRAMATIC MOMENTS

from the Major Plays

These short excerpts are from the playwright's major plays. They give a taste of the work of the playwright. Each has a short introduction in brackets that helps the reader understand the context of the excerpt. The excerpts, which are in chronological order, illustrate the main themes mentioned in the In an Hour essay. Premiere date is given.

CHARACTERS

Troy
Rose
Gabriel
Cory

[Troy Maxim and his wife Rose have been facing some difficult times. Troy is frustrated with the circumstances of his life and eager to re-energize himself. Additionally, he has been challenged by his teenage son, who is experimenting with his own manhood. In this scene, Troy brings devastating news to Rose. The arrival of Troy's troubled brother, Gabriel, and then Troy's son, Cory, only complicates this confrontation.]

(*Troy and his friend Bono have been working in Troy's yard. Bon has left and Troy's wife Rose has come out to bring him in for dinner.*)

TROY: Rose . . . I got something to tell you.

ROSE: Well, come on . . . wait till I get this food on the table.

TROY: Rose! (*She stops and turns around.*) I don't know how to say this. (*Pause.*) I can't explain it none. It just sort of grows on you till it gets out of hand. It starts out like a little bush . . . and the next thing you know it's a whole forest.

ROSE: Troy . . . what is you talking about?

TROY: I'm talking, woman, let me talk. I'm trying to find a way to tell you. . . I'm gonna be a daddy. I'm gonna be somebody's daddy.

ROSE: Troy . . . you're not telling me this? You're gonna be . . . what?

TROY: Rose . . now . . . see . . .

ROSE: You telling me you gonna be somebody's daddy? You telling your *wife* this?

(Gabriel enters from the street. He carries a rose in his hand.)

GABRIEL: Hey, Troy! Hey, Rose!

ROSE: I have to wait eighteen years to hear something like this.

GABRIEL: Hey, Rose . . . I got a flower for you. *(He hands it to her.)* That's a rose. Same rose like you is.

ROSE: Thanks, Gabe.

GABRIEL: Troy, you ain't mad at me is you? Them bad mens come and put me away. You ain't mad at me is you?

TROY: Naw, Gabe, I ain't mad at you.

ROSE: Eighteen years and you wanna come with this.

GABRIEL: *(Takes a quarter out of his pocket.)* See what I got? Got a brand new quarter.

TROY: Rose . . . it's just . . .

ROSE: Ain't nothing you can say, Troy. Ain't no way of explaining that.

GABRIEL: Fellow that give me this quarter had a whole mess of them. I'm gonna keep this quarter till it stop shining.

ROSE: Gabe, go on in the house there. I got some watermelon in the Frigidaire. Go on and get you a piece.

GABRIEL: Say, Rose . . . you know I was chasing hellhounds and them bad mens come and get me and take me away. Troy helped me. He come down there and told them they better let me go before he beat them up. Yeah, he did!

ROSE: You go on and get you a piece of watermelon, Gabe. Them bad mens is gone now.

GABRIEL: Okay, Rose . . . gonna get me some watermelon. The kind with the stripes on it.

(Gabriel exits into the house.)

ROSE: Why, Troy? Why? After all these years to come dragging this in to me now. It don't make no sense at your age. I could have expected this ten or fifteen years ago, but not now.

TROY: Age ain't got nothing to do with it, Rose.

ROSE: I done tried to be everything a wife should be. Everything a wife

could be. Been married eighteen years and I got to live to see the day
you tell me you been seeing another woman and done fathered a
child by her. And you know I ain't never wanted no half nothing in
my family. My whole family is half. Everybody got different fathers
and mothers . . . my two sisters and my brother. Can't hardly tell
who's who. Can't never sit down and talk about Papa and Mama.
It's your papa and your mama and my papa and my mama . . .

TROY: Rose . . . stop it now.

ROSE: I ain't never wanted that for none of my children. And now you
wanna drag your behind in here and tell me something like this.

TROY: You ought to know. It's time for you to know.

ROSE: Well, I don't want to know, goddamn it!

TROY: I can't just make it go away. It's done now. I can't wish the cir-
cumstance of the thing away.

ROSE: And you don't want to either. Maybe you want to wish me and
my boy away. Maybe that's what you want? Well, you can't wish us
away. I've got eighteen years of my life invested in you. You ought
to have stayed upstairs in my bed where you belong.

TROY: Rose . . . now listen to me . . . we can get a handle on this thing.
We can talk this out . . . come to an understanding.

ROSE: All of a sudden it's "we." Where was "we" at when you was down
there rolling Around with some godforsaken woman? "We" should
have come to an understanding before you started making a damn
fool of yourself. You're a day late and a dollar short when it comes
to an understanding with me.

TROY: It's just . . . She gives me a different idea . . . a different understanding about myself. I can step out of this house and get away
from the pressures and problems . . . be a different man. I ain't got
to wonder how I'm gonna pay the bills or get the roof fixed. I can
just be a part of myself that I ain't never been.

ROSE: What I want to know . . . is do you plan to continue seeing her?
That's all you can say to me.

TROY: I can sit up in her house and laugh. Do you understand what I'm saying? I can laugh out loud . . . and it feels good. It reaches all the way down to the bottom of my shoes. *(Pause.)* Rose, I can't give that up.

ROSE: Maybe you ought to go on and stay down there with her . . . if she a better woman than me.

TROY: It ain't about nobody being a better woman or nothing. Rose, you ain't the blame. A man couldn't ask for no woman to be a better wife than you've been. I'm responsible for it. I done locked myself into a pattern trying to take care of you all that forgot about myself.

ROSE: What the hell was I there for? That was my job, not somebody else's.

TROY: Rose, I done tried all my life to live decent . . . to live a clean . . . hard . . . useful life. I tried to be a good husband to you. In every way I knew how. Maybe come into the world backwards, I don't know. But . . . you born with two strikes on you before you come to the plate. You got to guard it closely . . . always looking for the curve ball on the inside corner. You can't afford to let none get past you. You can't afford a call strike. If you going down . . . you going down swinging. Everything lined up against you. What you gonna do? I fooled them, Rose. I bunted. When I found you and Cory and a halfway decent job . . . I was safe. Couldn't nothing touch me. I wasn't gonna strike out no more. I wasn't going back to the penitentiary. I wasn't gonna lay in the streets with a bottle of wine. I was safe. I had me a family. A job. I wasn't gonna get that last strike. I was on first looking for one of them boys to knock me in. To get me home.

ROSE: You should have stayed in my bed, Troy.

TROY: Then when I saw that gal . . . she firmed up my backbone. And I got to thinking that if I tried . . . I just might be able to steal second. Do you understand after eighteen years I wanted to steal second?

ROSE: You should have held me tight. You should have grabbed me and held on.

TROY: I stood on first base for eighteen years and I thought . . . well, goddamn it . . . go on for it!

ROSE: We're not talking about baseball! We're talking about you going off to lay in bed with another woman . . . and then bring it home to me. That's what we're talking about. We ain't talking about no baseball.

TROY: Rose, you're not listening to me. I'm trying the best I can to explain it to you. It's not easy for me to admit that I been standing in the same place for eighteen years.

ROSE: I been standing with you! I been right here with you, Troy. I got a life too. I gave eighteen years of my life to stand in the same spot with you. Don't you think I ever wanted other things? Don't you think I had dreams and hopes? What about my life? What about me? Don't you think it ever crossed my mind to want to know other men? That I wanted to lay up somewhere and forget about my responsibilities? That I wanted someone to make me laugh so I could feel good? You not the only one who's got wants and needs. But I held on to you, Troy. I took all my feelings, my wants and needs, my dreams . . . and I buried them inside you. I planted a seed and watched and prayed over it. I planted myself inside you and waited to bloom. And it didn't take me no eighteen years to find out the soil was hard and rocky and it wasn't never gonna bloom.

But I held on to you, Troy. I held you tighter. You was my husband. I owed you everything I had. Every part of me I could find to give you. And upstairs in that room . . . with the darkness falling in on me . . . I gave everything I had to try and erase the doubt that you wasn't the finest man in the world. And wherever you was going . . . I wanted to be there with you. Cause you was my husband. Cause that's the only way I was gonna survive as your wife. You always talking about what you give . . . and what you don't have to give. But you take, too. You take . . . and don't even know nobody's giving!

(Rose turns to exit into the house; Troy grabs her arm.)

TROY: You say I take and don't give!

ROSE: Troy! You're hurting me!

TROY: You say I take and don't give.

ROSE: Troy . . . you're hurting my arm! Let go!

TROY: I done give you everything I got. Don't you tell that lie on me.

ROSE: Troy!

TROY: Don't you tell that lie on me!

(Cory enters from the house.)

CORY: Mama!

ROSE: Troy. You're hurting me.

TROY: Don't you tell me about no taking and giving.

(Cory comes up behind Troy and grabs him. Troy, surprised, is thrown off balance just as Cory throws a glancing blow that catches him on the chest and knocks him down. Troy is stunned, as is Cory.)

ROSE: Troy. Troy. No!

(Troy gets to his feet and starts at CORY.)

ROSE: Troy . . . no. Please! Troy!

(Rose pulls on Troy to hold him back. Troy stops himself.)

TROY: *(To Cory.)* Alright. That's strike two. You stay away from around me, boy. Don't you strike out. You living with a full count. Don't you strike out.

(Troy exits out of the yard and the lights go down.)

****

from Joe Turner's Come and Gone (1988)
from Act Two, Scene 5

CHARACTERS

> Bynum
>
> Bertha
>
> Harold Loomis
>
> Bertha
>
> Zonia
>
> Mattie
>
> Seth
>
> Martha Loomis
>
> Rutherford Selig

[This final scene takes place in Bertha and Seth's boarding house where Herald Loomis and his daughter have been staying for two weeks. He has been waiting for the return of Rutherford Selig, a People Finder, who is helping Loomis reunite with his wife. Loomis lost contact with her after a period of forced servitude to the infamous Joe Turner.]

(The lights come up on the kitchen. It is Saturday. Bynum, Loomis, and Zonia sit atthe table. Bertha prepares breakfast. Zonia has on a white dress.)

BYNUM: With all this rain we been having he might have run into some washed-out roads. If that wagon got stuck in the mud, he's liable to be still upriver somewhere. If he's upriver then he ain't coming back until tomorrow.

LOOMIS: Today's Saturday. He say he be here on Saturday.

BERTHA: Zonia, you gonna eat your breakfast this morning.

ZONIA: Yes, ma'am.

BERTHA: I don't know how you expect to get any bigger if you don't eat. I aint' never seen a child that didn't eat. You about as skinny as a beanpole. *(Pause.)* Mr. Loomis, there's a place down on Wylie. Zeke Mayweather got a house down there. You ought to see if got any rooms. *(Loomis doesn't respond.)* Well, you're welcome to some breakfast before you move on.

(Mattie enters form the stairs.)

MATTIE: Good morning.

BERTHA: Morning, Mattie. Sit on down there and get you some breakfast.

BYNUM: Well, Mattie Campbell, you been sleeping with that up under your pillow like I told you?

BERTHA: Bynum, I don't told you to leave that gal alone with all that stuff. You around here meddling in other people's lives. She don't want to hear all that. You ain't doing nothing but confusing her with that stuff.

MATTIE: *(To Loomis.)* You all fixing to move on?

LOOMIS: Today's Saturday. I'm paid up till Saturday.

MATTIE: Where you going to?

LOOMIS: Gonna find my wife.

MATTIE: You going off to another city?

LOOMIS: We gonna see where the road take us. Ain't no telling where we wind up.

MATTIE: Eleven years is a long time. Your wife . . .she might have taken up with someone else. People do that when they get lost from each other.

LOMIS: Zonia. Come on, we gonna find your mama.

(Loomis and Zonia cross to the door.)

MATTIE: *(To Zonia.)* Zonia, Mattie got a ribbon here match your dress. Want Mattie to fix your hair with her ribbon?

(Zonia nods. Mattie fixes the ribbon in her hair.)

MATTIE: *(To Loomis.)* I hope you find her. I hope you be happy.

LOOMIS: A man looking for a woman be lucky to find you. You a good woman,

MATTIE: Keep a good heart.

(Loomis and Zonia exit.)

BERTHA: I been watching that man for two weeks . . . and that's the closest I come to seeing him act civilized. I don't know what's between you all, Mattie . . . but the only thing that man needs is somebody to make him laugh. That's all you need in the world is love and laughter. That's all anybody needs. To have love in one hand and laughter in the other. *(Bertha moves about the kitchen as though blessing it and chasing away the huge sadness that seems to envelop it. It is a dance and demonstration of her own magic, her own remedy that is centuries old and to which she is connected by the muscles of her heart and the blood's memory.)* You hear me, Mattie? I'm talking about laughing. The kind of laugh that comes from way deep inside. To just stand and laugh and let life flow right through you. Just laugh to let yourself know you're alive. *(She begins to laugh. It is a near-hysterical laughter that is a celebration of life, both its pain and its blessing. Mattie and Bynum join in the laughter. Seth enters from the front door.)*

SETH: Well, I see you all having fun. *(Seth begins to laugh with them.)* That Loomis fellow standing up there on the corner watching the house. He standing right up there on Manila Street.

BERTHA: Don't you get started on him. The man done left out of here and that's the last I wanna hear of it. You about to drive me crazy with that man.

SETH: I just say he standing up there on the corner. Acting sneaky like he always do. He can stand up there all he want. As long as he don't come back in here.

(There is a knock on the door. Seth goes to answer it. Enter Martha Loomis [PENTECOST]. She is a young woman about twenty-eight. She is dressed as befitting a member of an Evangelist church. Rutherford Selig follows.)

SETH: Look here, Bertha. It's Martha Pentecost. Come on in, Martha. Who that with you? Oh . . . that's Selig. Come on in, Selig.

BERTHA: Come on in, Martha. It's sure good to see you.

BYNUM: Rutherford Selig, you a sure enough first-class People Finder!

SELIG: She was right out there in Rankin. You take that first right-hand road . . . right there at that church on Wooster Street. I started to go right past and something told me to stop at the church and see if they needed any dustpans.

SETH: Don't she look good, Bertha.

BERTHA: Look all nice and healthy.

MARTHA: Mr. Bynum . . . Selig told me my little girl was here.

SETH: There's some fellow around here say he your husband. Say his name is Loomis. Say you his wife.

MARTHA: Is my little girl with him?

SETH: Yeah, he got a little girl with him. I wasn't gonna tell him where you was.

Not the way this fellow look. So he got Selig to find you.

MARTHA: Where they at? They upstairs?

SETH: He was standing right up there on Manila Street. I had to ask him to leave cause of how he was carrying on. He come in here one night

(The door opens and Loomis and Zonia enter. Martha and Loomis stare at each other.)

LOOMIS: Hello, Martha.

MARTHA: Herald . . . Zonia?

LOOMIS: You ain't waited for me, Martha. I got out the place looking to see your face. Seven years I waited to see your face.

MARTHA: Herald, I been looking for you. I wasn't but two months behind you when you went to my mama's and got Zonia. I been looking for you ever since.

LOOMIS: Joe Turner let me loose and I felt all turned around inside. I just wanted to see your face to know that the world was still there.

Make sure everything still in its place so I could reconnect myself together. I got there and you was gone, Martha.

MARTHA: Herald . . .

LOOMIS: Left my little girl motherless in the world.

MARTHA: I didn't leave her motherless, Herald. Reverend Tolliver wanted to move the church up North cause of all the trouble the colored folks was having down there. Nobody knew what was gonna happen traveling them roads. We didn't even know if we was gonna make it up here or not. I left her with my mama so she be safe. That was better than dragging her out on the road having to duck and hide from people. Wasn't no telling what was gonna happen to us. I didn't leave her motherless in the world. I been looking for you.

LOOMIS: I come up on Henry Thompson's place after seven years of living in hell, and all I'm looking to do is see your face.

MARTHA: Herald, I didn't know if you was ever coming back. They told me Joe Turner had you and my whole world split half in two. My whole life shattered. It was like I had poured it in a cracked jar and it all leaked out the bottom. When it go like that there ain't nothing you can do to put it back together. You talking about Henry Thompson's place like I'm still gonna be working the land by myself. How I'm gonna do that? You wasn't gone but two months and Henry Thompson kicked me off his land and I ain't had no place to go but to my mama's. I stayed and waited there for five years before I woke up one morning and decided that you was dead. Even if you weren't, you was dead to me. I wasn't gonna carry you with me no more. So I killed you in my heart. I buried you. I mourned you. And then I picked up what was left and went on to make life without you. I was a young woman with life at my beckon. I couldn't drag you behind me like a sack of cotton.

LOOMIS: I just been waiting to look on your face to say my goodbye. That good-bye got so big at times, seem like it was gonna swallow me up. Like Jonah in the whale's belly I sat up in that good-bye for three years. That good-bye kept me out on the road searching. Not looking on women in their houses. It kept me bound up to the road. All the time that good-bye swelling up in my chest till I'm about to bust. Now that I see your face I can say my good-bye and make my own world. *(Loomis takes Zonia's hand and presents her to Martha.)* Martha . . . here go your daughter. I tried to take care of her. See that she had something to eat. See that she was out of the elements. Whatever I know I tried to teach her. Now she need to learn from her mother whatever you got to teach her. That way she won't be no one-sided person. *(Loomis stoops to Zonia.)* Zonia, you go live with your mama. She a good woman. You go on with her and listen to her good. You my daughter and I love you like a daughter. I hope to see you again in the world somewhere. I'll never forget you.

ZONIA: *(Throws her arms around Loomis in a panic.)* I won't get no bigger! My bones won't get no bigger! They won't! I promise! Take me with you till we keep searching and never finding. I won't get no bigger! I promise!

LOOMIS: Go on and do what I told you now.

MARTHA: *(Goes to Zonia and comforts her.)* It's alright, baby. Mama's here. Mama's here. Don't worry. Don't cry. *(Martha turns to Bynum.)* Mr. Bynum, I don't know how to thank you. God bless you.

LOOMIS: It was you! All the time it was you that bind me up! You bound me to the road!

BYNUM: I ain't bind you, Herald Loomis. You can't bind what don't cling.

LOOMIS: Everywhere I go people wanna bind me up. Joe Turner wanna bind me up! Reverend Tolliver wanna bind me up. You wanna bind me up. Everybody wanna bind me up. Well, Joe Turner's come and gone and Herald Loomis ain't for no binding. I ain't gonna let nobody bind me up! *(Loomis pulls out a knife.)*

BYNUM: It wasn't you, Herald Loomis. I ain't bound you. I bound the little girl to her mother. That's who I bound. You binding yourself. You bound onto your song. All you got to do is stand up and sing it, Herald Loomis. It's right there kicking at your throat. All you got to do is sing it. Then you be free.

MARTHA: Herald . . . look at yourself! Standing there with a knife in your hand. You done gone over to the devil. Come on . . . put down the knife. You got to look to Jesus. Even if you done fell away from the church you can be saved again. The Bible say, "The Lord is my shepherd I shall not want. He maketh me to lie down in green pastures. He leads me beside the still water. He restoreth my soul. He leads me in the path of righteousness for His name's sake. Even though I walk through the shadow of death —"

LOOMIS: That's just where I be walking!

MARTHA: "I shall fear no evil. For thou art with me. Thy rod and thy staff, they comfort me."

LOOMIS: You can't tell me nothing about no valleys. I done been all across the valleys and the hills and the mountains and the oceans.

MARTHA: "Thou preparest a table for me in the presence of my enemies."

LOOMIS: And all I seen was a bunch of niggers dazed out of their woolly heads. And

Mr. Jesus Christ standing there in the middle of them, grinning.

MARTHA: "Thou annointest my head with oil, my cup runneth over."

LOOMIS: He grin that big old grin . . . and niggers wallowing at his feet.

MARTHA: "Surely goodness and mercy shall follow me all the days of my life, and I shall dwell in the house of the Lord forever."

LOOMIS: Great big old white man . . . your Mr. Jesus Christ. Standing there with a whip in one hand and tote board in another, and them niggers swimming in a sea of cotton. And he counting. He tallying up the cotton. "Well, Jeremiah . . . what's the matter, you ain't picked but two hundred pounds of cotton today? Got to put you on half rations." And Jeremiah go back and lay up there on his half rations and talk about what a nice man Mr. Jesus Christ is cause he give him salvation after he die. Something wrong here. Something don't fit right!

MARTHA: You got to open up your heart and have faith, Herald. This world is just a trial for the next. Jesus offers you salvation.

LOOMIS: I been wading in the water. I been walking all over the River

Jordan. But what it get me, huh? I done been baptized with blood of the lamb and the fire of the Holy Ghost. But what I got, huh? I got salvation? My enemies all around me picking the flesh from my bones. I'm choking on my own blood and all you got to give me is salvation?

MARTHA: You got to be clean, Herald. You got to be washed with the blood of the lamb.

LOOMIS: Blood make you clean? You clean with blood?

MARTHA: Jesus bled for you. He's the Lamb of God who takest away the sins of the world.

LOOMIS: I don't need nobody to bleed for me! I can bleed for myself.

MARTHA: You got to be something, Herald. You just can't be alive. Life don't mean nothing unless it got a meaning.

LOOMIS: What kind of meaning you got? What kind of clean you got, woman? You want blood? Blood make you clean? You clean with blood? *(Loomis slashes himself across the chest. He rubs the blood over his face and comes to a realization.)* I'm standing! I'm standing! My legs stood up! I'm standing now!

(Having found his song, the song of self-sufficiency, fully resurrected, cleansed and given breath, free from any encumbrance other than the workings of his own heart and the bonds of the flesh, having accepted the responsibility for his own presence in the world, he is free to soar above the environs that weighed and pushed his spirit into terrifying contractions.)

LOOMIS: Good-bye, Martha.

(Loomis turns and exits, the knife still in his hands. Mattie looks about the room and rushes out after him.)

BYNUM: Herald Loomis, you shining! You shining like new money!

(The lights go down to black.)

****

from **Two Trains Running** (1993)
from Act One, Scene 2

CHARACTERS

Memphis
Wolf
Risa
Holloway

[As the characters gather in Memphis Lee's diner, they discuss the actions of Hambone, a man wronged long ago in a business deal in which he was never paid what he was owed.]

(The lights come up on the restaurant. Wolf is looking out the window of the door. Memphis is at the end of the counter. Risa is in the back. "229" is written on the board.)

WOLF: Here he come now. Lutz coming down the street. Hambone standing there.

(Memphis comes around the corner of the counter and walks to the door and looks out.)

MEMPHIS: What's Holloway doing?

WOLF: He watching him. He just standing there. He wanna hear what they say. Look at him . . . look at him. Look at Hambone.

RISA: *(Entering form the back)* What you all looking at?

WOLF: We watching Hambone. We want to see what he say to Lutz. Holloway went over there to stand on the corner. Hambone talking to Lutz now.

MEMPHIS: That's the damnedest thing I ever seen. *(He walks back around the counter.)* Risa, you been here for a half an hour and ain't got the coffee on. What you doing back there? Get them grits cooked up. I told you put the bread in the refrigerator . . . keep it fresh.

WOLF: Lutz going in his store. He turned his back to him and opening up his store. Holloway still standing there. (*Turning from the window.*) Lutz ought to go on and give him a ham.

MEMPHIS: Lutz ain't gonna give him no ham . . . cause he don't feel he owe him. I wouldn't give him one either.

WOLF: After all this time it don't make no difference. He ought to go on and give him a ham. What difference to it make? It ain't like he ain't got none. Got a whole store full of hams.

MEMPHIS: What you do with that flour? Ain't even got the oven turned on. How you gonna cook biscuits without turning on the oven? Where's the flour? I bought ten pounds of flour yesterday.

RISA: It's in the back.

MEMPHIS: Here's the sifter. Sift the baking soda and flour together. You ain't used this sifter in a month. And get on up to the bakery and get West his pie before he gets over here.

WOLF: I heard tell somebody tried to break in West's last night to steal Prophet Samuel's money and jewels. Set off the burglar alarm . . . woke West up.

(*Holloway enters.*)

Hey, Holloway. We was watching you. What Hambone say? We seen Lutz when he come down the street. What he say?

HOLLOWAY: He told him he wanted his ham, that's all. Said, "I want my ham." Lutz told him, "Take a chicken," then he went on in his store. That was it. He ain't said nothing back to him. The only words exchanged was "I want my ham," and "Take a chicken."

MEMPHIS: I would just like to know . . . after nine and a half years . . . am I right, Holloway? . . . after nine and a half years . . . everyday . . . I wish my arithmetic was right to tell you how many days that is . . . nine and a half years . . . everyday . . . how . . . in his right mind . . .

do he think Lutz is gonna give him his ham? You answer me that. That's all I want to know.

WOLF: Anybody can see he ain't in his right mind.

HOLLOWAY: I don't know. He might be more in his right mind than you are. He might have more sense than any of us.

WOLF: Would you stand over there every morning for nine and a half years?

HOLLOWAY: I ain't saying that. Naw . . . hell, no . . . I wouldn't stand over there for nine and a half years. But maybe I ain't got as much sense as he got.

MEMPHIS: You tell me how that make sense. You tell me what sense that make?

HOLLOWAY: Alright. I'll tell you. Now you take me or you. We ain't gonna do that. We night take a chicken. Then we gonna go home and cook that chicken. But how it gonna taste? It can't taste good to us. We gonna beating just be eating. How we gonna feel good about ourselves? Every time we even look at a chicken we gonna have a bad taste in our mouth. That chicken's gonna call up that taste. It's gonna make you feel ashamed. Even if it be walking around flapping its wings its' gonna remind us of that bad taste. We ain't gonna tell nobody about it. We don't want nobody to know. But you can't erase it. You got to carry it around with you. This fellow here . . . he say he don't want to carry it around with him. But he ain't filling to forget about it. He trying to put the shame on the other foot. He trying to shame Lutz into giving him his ham. And if Lutz ever break down and give it to him . . . he gonna have a big thing. He gonna have something he be proud to tell everybody. He gonna tell his grandkids if he have any. That's why I say he might have more sense than me and you. Cause he ain't willing to accept whatever the white man throw at him. It be easier. But he say he don't mind getting out of bed in the morning to go at what's right. I don't believe you and me got that much sense.

****

CHARACTERS

Tonya

King Hedley

[King Hedley and his wife Tonya argue about her having the baby she is carrying. Finally, she explodes, sharing with him her reasons for not wanting to bring a child into this world.]

TONYA: . . . I ain't raising no kid to have somebody shoot him. To have his friends shoot him. To have the police shoot him. Why I want to bring another life into this world that don't respect life? I don't want to raise no more babies when you got to fight to keep them alive. You take Little Buddy Will's mother up on Bryn Mawr Road. What she got? A heartache that don't never go away. She up there now sitting down in her living room. She got to sit down 'cause she can't stand up. She sitting down trying to figure it out. Trying to figure out what happened. One minute her house is full of life. The next minute it's full of death. She was waiting for him to come home and they bring her a corpse. Say, "Come down and make the identification. Is this your son?" Got a tag on his toe say "John Doe." They got to put a number on it. "John Doe number four." She got the dinner on the table. Say, "Junior like fried chicken." She got some of that. Say "Junior like string beans." She got some of that. She don't know Junior ain't eating no more. He got a pile of clothes she washing up. She don't know Junior don't need no more clothes. She look in the closet. Junior ain't got no suit. She got to go buy him a suit. He can't try it on. She got to guess the size. Somebody come up and tell her, "Miss So-and-So, your boy got shot." She know before they say it. Her knees start to get weak. She shaking her head.

She don't want to hear it. Somebody call the police. They come and pick him up off the sidewalk. Dead nigger on Bryn Mawr Road. They got to quit playing cards and come and pick him up. They used to take pictures. The don't even take pictures no more. They pull him out of the freezer and she look at him. Don't want to look. They make her look. What to do now. The only thing to do is call the undertaker. The line is busy. She got to call back five times. The undertaker got so much business he don't know what to do. He losing sleep. He got to hire two more helpers to go with the two he already got. He don't even look at the bodies no more. He couldn't tell you what they look like. He only remembers the problems he have with them. This one so big and fat if he fall of the table it take six men to pick him up. That one ain't got no cheek. The one eyes won't say closed. The other one been dead so long he got maggots coming out of his nose. The family can't pay for that one. The coroner wants to tee the other one again. That one's mother won't go home. The other one . . . (*She stops to catch her breath.*) I ain't' going through that. I ain't having this baby . . . and I ain't got to explain it to nobody.

****

from **Gem of the Ocean** (2006)
from Act One, Scene 1

CHARACTERS

Eli
Black Mary
Rutherford Selig
Solly
Aunt Ester

[This opening scene introduces Aunt Ester, a character who recurs throughout the Wilson canon. Here, she arrives later in the scene — after the conflict around that the play rotates has been presented.]

The lights come up on Eli and Black Mary in the kitchen. They have just finished breakfast. Eli stands at the window looking out.

ELI: He still standing there. He been standing there since he left out of here yesterday. Aunt Ester told him she'd see him on Tuesday and he went and stood across the street there. I don't know what he want to see her about. He went right out there and stood across the street. If he go somewhere he come right back. He been out there every time I look.

BLACK MARY: Who is he?

ELI: He didn't say. He just say he wanted to see Aunt Ester. He look like he just come up here. He still wearing clodhoppers.

BLACK MARY: If he been standing over there he must not have nowhere to go.

ELI: He can go somewhere and sit down. Today's Saturday. Tuesday's a long way to go. Unless he gonna sleep standing up.

BLACK MARY: He waiting to see if Aunt Ester come out.

ELI: He gonna have a long wait. I ain't know her to leave the house in the past twenty years.

BLACK MARY: He probably go down under the Brady Street Bridge to sleep. They got a whole bunch of people sleeping down there.

ELI: They gonna have some more the way Caesar keep evicting people. He put out two more families yesterday. He charging by the week. They get one week behind and he put them out. He don't ask no questions. He just gather up what little bit of stuff they got and sit it out on the street. Then he arrest them for being out there. What Aunt Ester say?

BLACK MARY: She say no. I asked her if she wanted to get up she say no. I asked her if she was sick she say no.

ELI: It's going on four days now. I ain't never know her to sleep that long. Long as I known her.

BLACK MARY: I asked her did she want anything to eat she say no.

(There is a knock at the door. Eli goes to answer it. Rutherford Selig enters. He is carrying a frying pan and a can of kerosene.)

ELI: Hey Selig, come on in.

SELIG: Hey Eli. Here's your kerosene. I got your rocks on the wagon. Say Black Mary I got you that frying pan.

(Black Mary takes the frying pan and looks at it.)

SELIG: That's good iron. You can't get iron like that every day. That's high-grade iron. The bottom's nice and flat.

BLACK MARY: How much you gonna charge me? I paid too much for that coffeepot.

SELIG: I'll let you have it for two dollars. That's a three-dollar frying pan. For you it's two dollars. I would charge you fifty cents more but that's my last one like that and I'll be glad to get rid of it . . . get me a new order. You want the fourteen-inch? I'll have that next week.

BLACK MARY: I paid too much for that coffeepot. I don't want to pay too much for this frying pan.

SELIG: Well, how about dustpans? I'll let you have a dustpan with it for two dollars and twenty-five cents.

(Black Mary hesitates.)

SELIG: I'll tell you what. Make it the two dollars and I'll just give you the dustpan.

(Black Mary gives him two dollars.)

SELIG: Say Eli, I come from upriver. I see where they got the mill shut down.

ELI: They had a man named Garret Brown who jumped into the river. Caesar chased him and he jumped in and wouldn't come out. They say he stole a bucket of nails. He said he didn't do it. They having his funeral today.

SELIG: I seen the people standing around down at the church. They got a bunch of people standing around down there. I was wondering what they standing around there for.

ELI: They gonna bury him this afternoon. They gonna bury him out of Reverend Tolliver's church. They was supposed to bury him yesterday out of Reverend Flowers' church but Caesar stopped them. He went up to Reverend Flowers and told him it was against the law. The Christian law. Man ain't set foot in a church for thirty years talking about the Christian law. Caesar's just mad at him 'cause he didn't get a chance at him.

BLACK MARY: He could have come out of the water.

ELI: They couldn't get him to come out. Caesar told him he wasn't gonna arrest him. Told him he'd give him a bowl of soup and some dry clothes. He told Caesar to go to hell. Told his whole family to go to hell. He talking about you, Black Mary.

SELIG: You can't stay in there but so long. That cold will get to you and shut your body down.

ELI: He just treading water. Holding on to the barge. Caesar see he wasn't gonna come out he tried to beat him over the head with a two-by-four. Talking about he wasn't gonna do nothing to him. I believe he would have killed him right on the spot if he came out.

BLACK MARY: He wouldn't have done nothing but arrest him and the judge give him thirty days.

ELI: Well, as it is he dead.

SELIG: If he jumped in the river and didn't come out I'd have to believe he didn't do it. They had a man down in Kentucky was accused of stealing a horse. He said he didn't do it. Turned him into an outlaw. Made him the biggest horse thief in Kentucky. He lived to steal horses. He must of stole five hundred horses. And every one he sent back word: I stole that one but I didn't steal the first one. I stole that one but I didn't steal the first one. They never did catch him. He died and the horse thieving stopped. My daddy told me about it.

(There is a knock on the door. Eli goes to answer it. Solly enters singing "I Belong to the Band." He is sixty-seven years old. He wears a long coat and a battered hat. He carries a basket and a stick.)

SOLLY: (Singing.)
I belong to the band I belong to the band
I belong to the band, oh yes I do
Talking about that Railroad Band.

ELI: Hey Solly, come on in.

SOLLY: The people say they ain't going back to work at the mill. They lining up for the funeral down at the church. They lining up all around the block. Look like every Negro in Pittsburgh down there.

ELI: Reverend Tolliver's gonna get rich. The people appreciate him opening up his church.

BLACK MARY: Why don't you leave that basket outside? I told you leave it out there.

SOLLY: I'm afraid somebody's gonna run off with it.

BLACK MARY: Who's gonna steal a basket of dog shit?

SOLLY: It's pure! It's called pure! They got pure collectors all over the world. People been collecting pure for four hundred years.

BLACK MARY: I don't care what it's called. Who would want to steal it.

SOLLY: Anybody would steal it. Look here. (*Pulls some money out of his pocket.*) Where you think this come from? It come from this basket of pure. People will kill people over money. You know if they kill somebody over money they will steal anything that ain't nailed down.

BLACK MARY: Talking about somebody stealing a basket of dog shit.

SOLLY: A lot of people get confused by this pure. They don't know the shoemakers use it to work the leather. I had one old gal tell me, "Get on away from me you smell like dog shit." I showed her that two dollars I got from Butera and she told me come and go home with her. Cooked me up a whole pan of cornbread. I went on back up there and she was gone. I don't know what happened to her.

SELIG: There is a lot of them like that. Where you don't know what happened with them.

SOLLY: I do have my Special Rider though. She up on Webster. I'd marry her if I wasn't in love with somebody else.

BLACK MARY: Here, Selig. I baked you a loaf of bread.

SELIG: I thank you Black Mary. That way I won't have to stop by Caesar's bakery. I got to get on. I'll unload them rocks out back.

(Selig gets up to leave. Eli hands him two dollars.)

ELI: Thanks, Selig.

SELIG: If you need any more rocks you let me know. I can get you some cobblestones if you want.

ELI: Naw, I like the rocks.

SOLLY: Hey Selig. I see you got a new horse.

SELIG: Ain't she a beauty? Name's Sally. I got her from Jacob Herlich. He going up to New York to go in business with his brother.

SOLLY: Yeah, that's a nice-looking horse.

SELIG: I ain't had a speck of trouble out of her since I had her. I say get up and she go. Whoa and she stop. I feed her some oats and she carry me wherever I want to go. If everything go right I'm gonna get me a new wagon. See you next time, Black Mary. Tell Aunt Ester I asked about her.

BLACK MARY: Take care of yourself, Selig.

(Selig exits. Eli crosses back over to the window.)

ELI: Come on and help me build this wall.

SOLLY: Where you building a wall at?

ELI: Out back. I'm gonna take and build a wall around the side there.

SOLLY: You can get you some wood and build you a fence.

ELI: I want a wall.

SOLLY: I'll help you. When you wanna start?

ELI: Anytime you ready. We can start tomorrow.

SOLLY: All right.

ELI: I want a wall. See if I can keep Caesar on the other side. The way he going he gonna have everybody in jail.

BLACK MARY: Caesar's doing his job. That's what the people can't see.

SOLLY: Caesar's the kind of people I would want working for me. If I ever get me a plantation I'm gonna hire him to keep my niggers in line.

(Eli crosses to the window and looks out.)

SOLLY: I got a letter from my sister. Hey, Black Mary . . . read this for me. *(Hands her the letter.)*

BLACK MARY: *(Reads.)*

Dear Solomon,

I am writing to let you know the times are terrible here the most anybody remember since bondage. The people are having a hard time with freedom. I can't hold on here anymore. The white peoples is gone crazy and won't let anybody leave. They beat one fellow on the road so bad his mama say, "Who is he? They killed some more and say the colored can't buy any tickets on the train to get away. Say they will sink the ferry if any colored on it. I want to leave to come North but it is too bad. It is a hard time for everybody. Write and let me know what to do as I try to hold on but can't.

Your loving sister, Eliza Jackson

SOLLY: I got to go back down there.

ELI: I would go with you but I got to take care of Aunt Ester.

SOLLY: I got to go back down there and get my sister. I'm gonna see if Jefferson Culpepper wanna go with me.

ELI: I'm surprised Jefferson Culpepper can walk old as he is. You talking about eight hundred miles. Eight hundred miles one way is eight hundred miles coming back. He need to go find him a rocking chair somewhere.

SOLLY: I believe I can make it back down there if I don't get sleepy. I get sleepy sometime and don't know if I got it mixed up with the time and it really be night even though it look like the daytime. A lot of things can fool you like that. A lot of things shine like gold ain't gold. A lot of brass shine like gold.

(Aunt Ester enters.)

[When we return to the scene, Aunt Ester, who has been speaking with Solly and Eli, shares her dream.]

AUNT ESTER: . . . I had a dream about you last night.

SOLLY: My dreams won't stay in one place long enough for me to remember them.

AUNT ESTER: I dreamed you had a ship full of men and you was coming across the water. Had that stick and you was standing up in this boat full of men. You come and asked me what I was doing standing there. I told you I wanted to go back across the ocean. I asked you to take me. You said you had some work to do but that you would come back. Told me you had a magic stick and when you come back you would part the water so I could walk across. You come on back and all your men had drowned and the boat was sinking. You said you was going to get another boat and some more men. Said you would come back and smote the water. Then you walked off with that stick. Said you was going to Alabama.

SOLLY: I just got a letter from my sister today. I got to go! She say she can't hold on no more. Say the white people have gone crazy. I got to go back down there to get her. Eli say he staying here with you.

But I got to go get my sister. This my last trip. I'm getting old. I can't do more than one more. I don't know what I'm gonna do then. I was thinking about living my life for you. But I got to go back down there and get my sister.

(Eli enters from Aunt Ester's room.)

ELI: I got that stove working. Just leave it set like it is. If it get too hot in there let me know.

(Eli goes to the coat rack to get his coat and hat.)

Solly, you ready to go down to Garret Brown's funeral?

(Solly goes to get his coat and hat.)

AUNT ESTER: Come on back and get some of these pigfeet.
SOLLY: I want more than pigfeet. But I don't think you gonna give me none.
AUNT ESTER: Go on you old rascal you!

(Solly and Eli exit. The lights go down on the scene.)

****

A. Wilson

THE READING ROOM

YOUNG ACTORS AND THEIR TEACHERS

Bernstein, Richard. "August Wilson's Voices from the Past." *New York Times*, March 27, 1988, sec. 2.1, 34.

Bigsby, Christopher. "August Wilson: the Ground on Which He Stood." In *The Cambridge Companion to August Wilson*, edited by Christopher Bigsby. Cambridge: Cambridge University Press, 2007. 1–27.

Bloom, Harold, ed. *August Wilson*. Broomhall, Pa.: Chelsea House, 2002.

Bogumil, Mary L. *Understanding August Wilson*. Columbia: University of South Carolina Press, 1999.

Brantley, Ben. "The World That Created August Wilson." *New York Times*, March 27, 1988, sec. 2.1, 5.

Brown, Chip. "The Light in August." *Esquire*, April 1989, 116–25.

Harrison, Paul Carter, and Victor Leo Walker II, eds. "August Wilson's Call." Special issue, *African American Review* 31, no. 4 (1997).

Hay, Samuel. "*Joe Turner's Come and Gone.*" In *The Cambridge Companion to August Wilson*, edited by Christopher Bigsby. Cambridge: Cambridge University Press, 2007: 89–101.

Kroll, Jack. "August Wilson's Come to Stay." *Newsweek*, April II, 1988, 82.

Schwartzman, Myron. *Romare Bearden, His Life and Art*. New York: Harry Abrams, Inc. 1990

Snodgrass, Mary Ellen. *August Wilson: a Literary Companion*. Jefferson, N.C.: McFarland & Co., 2004.

Wallach, Allan. "Fenced in by a Lifetime of Resentments." *New York Newsday*, March 27, 1987. It was also published in *New York Theatre Critics Reviews,* 1987, 319.

Wilson, August. "Black Aesthetic: A Conversation with August Wilson." By Abiola Sinclair. In *Amsterdam News,* May 19, 1930.

This extensive bibliography lists books about the playwright according to whom the books might be of interest. If you would like to research further something that interests you in the text, lists of references, sources cited, and editions used in this book are found in this section.

Wilson, August. "August Wilson: Playwright." By Bill Moyers. *A World of Ideas*, New York: Doubleday, 1989: 167–80.

Wilson, August. "An Interview with August Wilson." By Yvonne Shafer. *Journal of Dramatic Theory and Criticism* 4 (fall 1989): 161–73.

Wilson, August. "The Historical Perspective." By Richard Pettengill. *August Wilson: A Casebook*, edited by Marilyn Elkins. New York: Garland, 1994: 235–54

Wilson, August. "August Wilson." By David Savran. *In Their Own Words: Contemporary American Playwrights*, New York: Theatre Communications Group, 1998: 288–305.

Wilson, August. "Homeward Bound: August Wilson." By Chris Jones. *American Theatre* 16, no. 9 (1999): 14–17.

Wilson, August. "An Interview with August Wilson." By Bonnie Lyons. *Contemporary Literature* 40, no. I (1999): I-21.

Wilson, August. "An Interview with August Wilson." By Herb Boyd. In *The Black World Today*, April 2000. www.tbwt.com/views/specialrpt/special%20report

Wilson, August. "An Interview with August Wilson." By Christopher Bigsby." *The Cambridge Companion to August Wilson*, edited by Christopher Bigsby. Cambridge: Cambridge University Press, 2007. 202–213

SCHOLARS, STUDENTS, PROFESSORS

Abbotson, Susan C. "From Jug Band to Dixieland: The Musical Development Behind August Wilson's Ma Rainey's Black Bottom." *Modern Drama* 43, no. I (2000): 100–108.

Anderson, Douglas. "Saying Goodbye to the Past: Self-Empowerment and History in Joe Turner's Come and Gone." *College Language Association Journal* 40, no. 4 (1997): 432–57.

Arnold, David L. G. "Seven Guitars: August Wilson's Economy of Blues." In *August Wilson: A Casebook*, edited by Marilyn Elkins. New York: Garland, 1994: 299–225.

Arthur, Thomas H. "Looking for My Relatives: The Political Implications of 'Family' in Selected Work of Athol Fugard and August Wilson." *South African Theatre* 6, no. 2 (1992): 5–16.

Awkward, Michael. "The Crooked and the Straights: Fences, Race, and the Politics of Adaptation." In *May All Your Fences Have Gates*, edited by Alan Nadel. Iowa City: University of Iowa Press, 1994: 104–29.

Bellamy, Lou. "The Colonization of Black Theatre." *African American Review* 31, no. 4 (1997): 587–94.

Bergesen, Eric, and William W. Demastes. "The Limits of African-American Political Realism: Baraka's Dutchman and Wilson's Ma Rainey's Black Bottom." In *Realism and the American Dramatic Tradition*, edited by William W. Demastes. Tuscaloosa: University of Alabama Press, 1996: 218–34.

Birdwell, Christine. "Death as a Fastball on the Outside Corner: Fences' Troy Maxson and the American Dream." *Aethlon* 8, no. 1 (1990): 87–96.

Bissiri, Amadou. "Aspects of Africanness in August Wilson's Drama: *Reading The Piano Lesson* through Wole Soyinka's Drama." *African American Review* 30, no. 1 (1996): 99–113.

Blumenthal, Anna S. "Joe Turner's Come and Gone: Sacrificial Rites and Rebirth of the Self.*" Postscript: Publication of the Philological Association of the Carolinas* 15 (1998): 53–65.

_____. "'More Stories Than the Devil Got Sinners': Troy's Stories in August Wilson's Fences." *American Drama* 9, no. 2 (2000): 74–96.

Boan, Devon, "Call-and-Response: Parallel 'Slave Narrative' in August Wilson's *The Piano Lesson*." *African American Review* 32, no. 2 (1998): 263–72.

Booker, Margaret. *Lillian Hellman and August Wilson: Dramatizing a New American Identity.* New York: Peter Lang, 2003.

_____. "*Radio Golf*: The Courage of his Convictions — Survival, Success and Spirituality." In *The Cambridge Companion to August Wilson*, edited by Christopher Bigsby. Cambridge: Cambridge University Press, 2007. 183–192.

Bottoms, Stephen. "*Two Trains Running*: Blood on the Tracks." In *The Cambridge Companion to August Wilson*, edited by Christopher Bigsby. Cambridge: Cambridge University Press, 2007. 145–157.

Brewer, Gaylord. "Holy and Unholy Ghosts: The Legacy of the Father in the Plays of August Wilson." In *Naming the Father: Legacies, Genealogies, and Explorations of Fatherhood in Modern and Contemporary Literature, edited by Eva Paulino Bueno, Terry Caesar, and William Hummel.* Lanham, Md.: Lexington Press, 2000: 120–39.

Clark, Keith. *Black Manhood in James Baldwin, Ernest J. Gaines, and August Wilson.* Urbana: University of Illinois Press, 2002.

Crawford, Eileen. "The Bb Burden: The Invisibility of Ma Rainey's Black Bottom." In *August Wilson: A Casebook*, edited by Marilyn Elkins. New York: Garland, 1994: 31–48.

Dorsey, John T. "African History in American Plays: August Wilson." In *Methods for the Study of Literature as Cultural Memory*, edited by Raymond Vervliet. Amsterdam: Rodopi, 2000: 362–67.

Dworkin, Norine. "Blood on the Tracks." *American Theater,* May 1990, 8.

——————. "August Wilson's Women." In *May All Your Fences Have Gates*, edited by Alan Nadel. Iowa City: University of Iowa Press, 1994: 167–82.

——————. "Of Angels and Transcendence: A Cross-Cultural Analysis of Fences by August Wilson and Roosters by Milcha Sanchez-Scott." In *Staging Difference: Cultural Pluralism in American Theatre*, edited by Marc Maufort, 287–300. New York: Peter Lang, 1995.

——————. "The Dialectics of August Wilson's Piano Lesson." *Theatre Journal* 52, no. 3 (2000): 362–79.

——————. "*Gem of the Ocean* and the Redemptive Power of History." In *The Cambridge Companion to August Wilson,* edited by Christopher Bigsby. Cambridge: Cambridge University Press, 2007: 75–88.

Fishman (Herrington), Joan. "Romare Bearden and August Wilson." In *May All Your Fences Have Gates*, edited by Alan Nadel. Iowa City: University of Iowa Press, 1994: 133–149.

Gantt, Patricia. "Ghosts from 'Down There': The Southernness of August Wilson." In *August Wilson: A Casebook*, edited by Marilyn Elkins, 69–88. New York: Garland, 1994.

Glover, Margaret E. "Two Notes on August Wilson: The Songs of a Marked Man." *Theater* 19, no. 3 (1988): 69–70.

Gordon, Joanne. "Wilson and Fugard." In *August Wilson: A Casebook*, edited by Marilyn Elkins, 17–29. New York: Garland, 1994.

Herrington, Joan. "*King Hedley II:* In the Midst of All This Death." In *The Cambridge Companion to August Wilson*, edited by Christopher Bigsby. Cambridge: Cambridge University Press, 2007: 169–182.

Joseph, May. "Alliances across the Margins." *African American Review* 31, no. 4 (1997): 595–99.

Keller, James R. "The Shaman's Apprentice: Ecstasy and Economy in Wilson's *Joe Turner*." *African American Review* 35, no. 3 (2001): 471–79.

Kester, Gunilla Theander. "Approaches to Africa: The Poetics of Memory and the Body in Two August Wilson Plays." In *August Wilson: A Casebook*, edited by Marilyn Elkins. New York: Garland, 1994: 105–121.

Krasner, David. "*Jitney,* Folklore and Responsibility." In *The Cambridge Companion to August Wilson*, edited by Christopher Bigsby. Cambridge: Cambridge University Press, 2007: 158–168.

Kubitschek, Missy Dean. "August Wilson's Gender Lesson." In *May All Your Fences Have Gates*, edited by Alan Nadel. Iowa City: University of Iowa Press, 1994: 183–199.

Lahr, John. "Been Here and Gone: How August Wilson Brought a Century of Black American Culture to the Stage." *New Yorker*, April 16, 2001, 50–65.

_____. "Been here and gone." In *The Cambridge Companion to August Wilson*, edited by Christopher Bigsby. Cambridge: Cambridge University Press, 2007: 28–51.

Londre, Felicia Hardison. "A Piano and Its History: Family and Transcending Family." In *The Cambridge Companion to August Wilson*, edited by Christopher Bigsby. Cambridge: Cambridge University Press, 2007. 113–123.

Marra, Kim. "Ma Rainey and the Boyz: Gender Ideology in August Wilson's Broadway Canon." In *August Wilson: A Casebook*, edited by Marilyn Elkins, 123–60. New York: Garland, 1994.

McDonough, Carla J. *Staging Masculinity: Male Identity in Contemporary American Drama*. Jefferson, N.C.: McFarland, 1997.

Monaco, Pamela Jean. "Father, Son, and Holy Ghost: From the Local to the Mythical in August Wilson." In *August Wilson: A Casebook*, edited by Marilyn Elkins. New York: Garland, 1994: 89–104.

Morales, Michael. "Ghosts on the Piano: August Wilson and the Representation of Black American History." In *May All Your Fences Have Gates*, edited by Alan Nadel. Iowa City: University of Iowa Press, 1994: 105–115.

Murphy, Brenda. "The Tragedy of *Seven Guitars*." In *The Cambridge Companion to August Wilson*, edited by Christopher Bigsby. Cambridge: Cambridge University Press, 2007. 124–134.

Nadel, Alan. "Boundaries, Logistics, and Identity: The Property of Metaphor in Fences and Joe Turner's Come and Gone." In *May All Your Fences Have Gates*, edited by Alan Nadel. Iowa City: University of Iowa Press, 1994: 86–104.

_____. "*Ma Rainey's Black Bottom Cutting the Historical Record.*" In *The Cambridge Companion to August Wilson*, edited by Christopher Bigsby. Cambridge: Cambridge University Press, 2007. 102–112.

Pereira, Kim. "Music and Mythology in August Wilson's Plays." In *The Cambridge Companion to August Wilson*, edited by Christopher Bigsby. Cambridge: Cambridge University Press, 2007. 65–74.

Pettengill, Richard. "Alternatives . . . Opposites . . . Convergences: An Interview with Lloyd Richards." In *August Wilson: A Casebook*, edited by Marilyn Elkins, 227–34. New York: Garland, 1994.

Richards, Sandra. "Yoruba Gods on the American Stage: August Wilson's *Joe Turner's Come and Gone.*" *Research in African Literatures* 30, no. 4 (1999): 92–105.

Roudane, Matthew. "Safe at Home? August Wilson's *Fences.*" In *The Cambridge Companion to August Wilson*, edited by Christopher Bigsby. Cambridge: Cambridge University Press, 2007: 135–144.

Sauer, David K. and Sauer, Janice A. "Critics on August Wilson." In *The Cambridge Companion to August Wilson*, edited by Christopher Bigsby. Cambridge: Cambridge University Press, 2007: 193–202.

Saunders, James Robert. "Essential Ambiguities in the Plays of August Wilson." *Hollins Critic* 32, no. 5 (1995): 1–12.

Shafer, Yvonne. "Breaking Barriers: August Wilson." In *Staging Difference: Cultural Pluralism in American Theatre*, edited by Marc Maufort. New York: Peter Lang, 1995: 267–85.

_____."August Wilson and the Contemporary Theatre." *Journal of Dramatic Theory and Criticism* 12 (fall 1997): 23–38.

_____. *August Wilson: A Research and Production Sourcebook*. Westport, Conn.: Greenwood Press, 1998.

Shannon, Sandra G. "The Good Christian's Come and Gone: The Shifting Role of Christianity in August Wilson's Plays." *Melus* 16, no. 3 (1989): 127–42.

_____. "The Ground on Which I Stand: August Wilson's Perspective on African American Women." In *May All Your Fences HaveGates*, edited by Alan Nadel. Iowa City: University of Iowa Press, 1994: 150–166.

_____. "The Role of Memory in August Wilson's Four-Hundred-Year Autobiography." In *Memory and Cultural Politics,* edited by Amritjit Singh, Joseph T. Skerret, Jr., and Robert E. Hogan, 175–93. Boston: Northeastern University Press, 1996.

_____. "A Transplant That Did Not Take: August Wilson's Views on the Great Migration." *African American Review* 31, no. 4 (1997): 659–66.

Smith, Philip E., II. "*Ma Rainey's Black Bottom*: Playing the Blues as Equipment for Living." In *Within the Dramatic Spectrum*, vol. 6, edited by Karelissa V. Hartigan, 177–86. New York: University Press of America, 1988.

Sterling, Eric. "Protecting Home: Patriarchal Authority in August Wilson's *Fences*." *Essays in Theatre/Etudes Theatrales* 17, no. 1 (1998): 53–62.

Timpane, John. "Filling the Time: Reading History in the Drama of August Wilson." In *May All Your Fences Have Gates*, edited by Alan Nadel. Iowa City: University of Iowa Press, 1994: 67–85.

Usekes, Cigdem. "'You Always under Attack': Whiteness as Law and Terror in August Wilson's Twentieth-Century Cycle of Plays." *American Drama* 10, no. 2 (2001): 48–68.

Wang, Qun. "Towards the Poetization of the Field of Manners." *African American Review* 29, no. 4 (1995): 605–13.

_____. *An In-Depth Study of the Major Plays of African American Playwright August Wilson: Vernacularizing the Blues on Stage.* Lewiston, N.Y.: Edwin Mellen Press, 1999.

Werner, Craig. "August Wilson's Burden: The Function of Neoclassical Jazz." In *May All Your Fences Have Gates*, edited by Alan Nadel. Iowa City: University of Iowa Press, 1994: 21–50.

Wilde, Lisa. "Reclaiming the Past: Narrative and Memory in August Wilson's *Two Trains Running*." *Theater* 22, no. I (1990): 73–74.

Williams, Dana A. "Making the Bones Live Again: A Look at the 'Bones People' in August Wilson's *Joe Turner's Come and Gone* and Henry Dumas's Ark of Bones." *College Language Association Journal* 41, no. 3 (1999): 309–19.

_____. "A Review Essay of Scholarly Criticism on the Drama of August Wilson." *Bonner Beitrage* 55, no. 2. (1998): 53–62.

Wilson, August. "August Wilson's Bottomless Blackness." By Michael Feingold. In *Village Voice*, 39 (27 November 1984), 117,118.

Wilson, August. "A Song in Search of Itself." By Hilary DeVries. *American Theatre* 3, no. 10 (1987): 25.

Wilson, August. "August Wilson." By John L. Di Gaetani. In *A Search for a Postmodern Theater: Interviews with Contemporary Playwrights.* Westport, Conn.: Greenwood Press, 1991.

Wilson, August. "A Conversation with August Wilson." By Dana Williams and Sandra Shannon. *August Wilson and Black Aesthetics.* New York: Palgrave Macmillan, 2004: 187–95.

THEATERS, PRODUCERS

Ambush, Benny Sato. "Culture Wars." *African American Review* 31, no. 4 (1997): 579–86.

Bogumil, Mary L. 'Tomorrow Never Comes': Songs of Cultural Identity in August Wilson's *Joe Turner's Come and Gone."* *Theatre Journal* 46, no. 4 (1994): 463–76.

_____. "August Wilson's Relationship to Black Theatre: Community, Aesthetics, History and Race." In *The Cambridge Companion to August Wilson*, edited by Christopher Bigsby. Cambridge: Cambridge University Press, 2007: 52–64.

Freedman, Samuel G. "A Playwright Talks about the Blues." *New York Times*, October 14, 1984, sec 12, 1.

_____."A Voice from the Streets." *New York Times Magazine*, March 15, 1987, 49.

Herrington, Joan. "Responsibility in Our Own Hands.*" Journal of Dramatic Theory and Criticism* 13, no. 1 (1998): 87–99.

Leverett, James, et al. "Beyond Black and White: 'Cultural Power': Thirteen Commentaries." *American Theater* 14, no. 5 (1997): 14–15, 53–56.

Moyers, Bill. "August Wilson." *A World of Ideas: Conversations with Thoughtful Men and Women about American Life Today and Ideas Shaping our Future.* Ed. Betty Sue Flowers. NewYork: Doubleday, 1989.

Pereira, Kim. *August Wilson and the African-American Odyssey.* Urbana: University of Illinois Press, 1995.

Reed, Ishmael. "In Search of August Wilson." *Connoisseur* 217 (March 1987): 92–97.

Shannon, Sandra G. "Audience and Africanisms in August Wilson's Dramaturgy: A Case Study." In *African American Performance and Theater History: A Critical Reader*, edited by Harry J. Elam and David Krasner, 149–67. Oxford: Oxford University Press, 2001.

Wilson, August. "Cool August: Mr. Wilson's Red-Hot Blues." By Dinah Livingston. *In Minnesota Monthly,* 21 (October 1987), 25–32.

Wilson, August. "Hurdling Fences." By Dennis Watlington. *Vanity Fair*, April 1989, 102–13.

Wilson, August. "A Conversation with August Wilson." By Mark William Rocha. *Diversity I* (fall 1992): 24-42.

Wilson, August. "August Wilson: Bard of the Blues." By Carol Rosen. In *Theater Week 9.* May 27, 1996: 18, 20, 22, 24–28, 30–32, 34–35.

ACTORS, DIRECTORS, PROFESSIONALS

Adell, Sandra. "Speaking of Ma Rainey/Talking about the Blues." In *May All Your Fences Have Gates*, edited by Alan Nadel. Iowa City: University of Iowa Press, 1994: 50–66.

Barbour, David. "August Wilson's Here to Stay." *Theater Week*, April 18–25, 1988, 8–14.

Ching, Mei-Lei. "Wrestling with History." *Theater* 20 (summer–fall 1988): 70–71.

Dworkin, Norine. "Ma Rainey's Black Bottom: Singing Wilson's Blues." *American Drama* 5, no. 2 (1996): 76–99.

Elkins, Marilyn, ed. *Wilson: A Casebook*. New York: Garland, 1994, 161–181.
Feingold, Michael. 1994. Unpublished Interview by Joan Herrington.

Fishman (Herrington), Joan. "Developing His Song: August Wilson's Fences." In *August Wilson: A Casebook*, edited by Marilyn Elkins, 161–181. New York: Garland, 1994.

Fleche, Anne. "The History Lesson: Authenticity and Anachronism in August Wilson's Plays." In *May All Your Fences Have Gates*, edited by Alan Nadel. Iowa City: University of Iowa Press, 1994: 9–20.

Goldberger, Paul. "From Page to Stage: Race and the Theater." *New York Times*, January 22, 1997, sec. C11, 14.

Harris, Trudier. "August Wilson's Folk Traditions." In *August Wilson: A Casebook*, edited by Marilyn Elkins, 49–67. New York: Garland, 1994.
_____. "The Crisis of Black Theatre Identity." *African American Review* 31, no. 4 (1997): 567–78.

Herrington, Joan. *"I Ain't Sorry for Nothin' I Done": August Wilson's Process of Playwriting*. New York: Limelight Editions, 1998.
_____. "On August Wilson's Jitney." American Drama 8, no. I (1998): 122–44.

Ivison, Douglas. "The Use and Abuse of History: A Naturalist Reading of August Wilson's The Piano Lesson." *Excavatio* 20 (2997): 9–20.

Plum, Jay. "Blues, History, and the Dramaturgy of August Wilson." *African American Review* 27, no. 4 (1993): 561–67.

Rocha, Mark William. "Black Madness in August Wilson's 'Down the Line' Cycle." In *Madness in Drama*, edited by James Redmond. Cambridge: Cambridge University Press, 1993: 191–201.

_____. "American History as 'Loud Talking' in *Two Trains Running*." In *May All Your Fences Have Gates*, edited by Alan Nadel. Iowa City: University of Iowa Press, 1994: 116–132.

_____. "August Wilson and the Four B's: Influences." In *August Wilson: A Casebook*, edited by Marilyn Elkins. New York: Garland, 1994: 3–16.

Shannon, Sandra G. "Conversing with the Past: *Joe Turner's Come and Gone and The Piano Lesson*." *CEA Magazine* 4, no. 1 (1991): 33–42.

_____. "The Long Wait: August Wilson's Ma Rainey's Black Bottom." *Black American Literature Forum* 23 (Spring 1991): 151–62

_____. "Subtle Imposition: The Lloyd Richards–August Wilson Formula." In *August Wilson: A Casebook*, edited by Marilyn Elkins, 183–98. New York: Garland, 1994.

_____. *The Dramatic Vision of August Wilson*. Washington, D.C.: HowardUniversity Press, 1995.

_____. *August Wilson's "Fences": A Reference Guide*. Westport, Conn.: Greenwood Press, 2003.

Tallmer, Jerry. "Hearing Voices," *Playbill* for *Two Trains Running*, April, 1991, p. 11–12.

Taylor, Regina. "That's Why They Call It the Blues." *American Theatre* 13, no. 4 (1996): 18–23.

Wessling, Joseph H. "Wilson's Fences." *Explicator* 57, no. 2. (1999): 123–127.

Wilson, August. "An Interview with August Wilson." By Kim Powers. *Theater* 16 (fall–winter 1984): 50-55.

Wilson, August. "August Wilson — a New Voice for Black American Theater." By Hilary DeVries. In *Christian Science Monitor* 18 (October 1984): 51-54.

Wilson, August. "Cool August: Mr. Wilson's Red-Hot Blues." By Dinah Livingston. In *Minnesota Monthly*, 21 (October 1987), 25–32.

Wilson, August. "Blues, History, and Dramaturgy." By Sandra G. Shannon. *African American Review* 27, no. 4 (1993): 539–59.

Wilson, August. "August Wilson" By Joan Herrington, unpublished interview with Michael Feingold, 1994.

Wilson, August. "August Wilson Explains his Dramatic Vision: An Interview." By Sandra Shannon In *Dramatic Vision of August Wilson*, Washington D.C.: Howard University Press, 1995: 201–35.

Wilson, August. "August Wilson Explains his Dramatic Vision: An Interview." By Sandra Shannon. In *Dramatic Vision of August Wilson*, Washington D.C.: Howard University Press, 1995: 201–35

Wilson, August. "Men, Women, and Culture: A Conversation with August
Wilson." By Nathan L. Grant. *American Drama* 5, no. 2 (1996):
100–122.

Wilson, August. "On Listening: An Interview with August Wilson." By Susan
Johann. *American Theatre* 13, no. 4 (1996): 22–23.

Wilson, August. "The Art of Theater XIV: August Wilson." By George
Plimpton and Bonnie Lyons. *Paris Review* 41, no. 153 (1999): 66–94.

Wilson, August. "August Wilson on Playwriting: An Interview." By Eliza-
beth J. Heard. *African American Review* 35, no. I (2001): 93–102.

THE EDITIONS OF AUGUST WILSON'S WORKS USED FOR THIS BOOK

Fences, Ma Rainey's Black Bottom, and Joe Turner's Come and Gone, contained in *August Wilson: Three Plays*. Pittsburgh: University of Pittsburgh Press, 1991.

Gem of the Ocean. New York: Theatre Communications Group, 2006.

The Homecoming (Unpublished property of August Wilson, nd)

The Janitor. In *Literature and Its Writers: An Introduction,* by Ann Charters
and Samuel Charters. Boston: Bedford, 1997

Jitney. Woodstock, New York: Overlook Press, 2001.

King Hedley II. New York: Theatre Communications Group, 2005.

The Piano Lesson. New York: Plume/Dutton, 1990.

Radio Golf. New York: Theatre Communications Group, 2007

Seven Guitars, New York: Plume/Dutton, 1997.

Two Trains Running. New York: Plume/Dutton, 1993.

SOURCES CITED IN THIS BOOK

Adcock, Joe. "August Wilson, 1945–2005: Playwright gave voice to black
experience." *The Seattle Post-Intelligencer*, October 5, 2005.

Asante, Molefi Kete, "The Future of African Gods: The Class of Civilizations, www.asante.net/news/ptare-accera-speech.html.

Brustein, Robert. "The Lesson of *The Piano Lesson*." *The New Republic*, May 21, 1990: 28–30.

Dutton, Charles, 1993. Unpublished interview with Joan Herrington.

Elam, Harry. "August Wilson, Doubling Madness, and Modern African-American Drama." *Modern Drama* 43, no. 4 (2000): 611–32.

_____. *Past as Present in the Drama of August Wilson*, Ann Arbor: University of Michigan Press, 2004.

Feingold, Michael. 1994. Unpublished interview with Joan Herrington.

Freedman, Samuel G. "A Playwright Talks about the Blues." *New York Times*, October 14, 1984, sec 12, 1.

Hampton, Aubrey. "August Wilson: Playwright," *Organica*, Summer, 1988: 24–27.

Harrison, Paul Carter. "August Wilson's Blues Poetics." In *Three Plays by August Wilson*. Pittsburgh: University of Pittsburgh Press, 1991, 191–317.

Kendt, Rob. "August Wilson," *Backstage West*, February 10, 2000: 8.

Rothstein, Mervyn. "Round Five for a Theatrical Heavyweight," *New York Times*, April 15, 1990, A&L: 1.

Tallmer, Jerry. "Hearing Voices," *Playbill* for *Two Trains Running*, April, 1991, 8–12.

Wilson, August. Forward to *Romare Beardon: His Life and Art*. Edited by Myron Schwartzman. New York: Harry Abrams, 1990.

_____." The Ground on Which I Stand." Keynote address to the Theatre Communications Group, June 26, 1996. *American Theatre* 13, no. 7 (1996): 14–17, 71–74.

_____. Preface to *August Wilson: Three Plays*. Pittsburgh: University of Pittsburgh Press, 1991.

_____. "August Wilson Responds." *American Theatre*, October 1996: 105–107.

_____. 1994. Unpublished interview with Joan Herrington.

Wolfe, Peter. *August Wilson*. New York: Twayne, 1999.

Awards

"AND THE WINNER IS . . ."

	PULITZER PRIZE	TONY AWARD	NY DRAMA CRITICS CIRCLE AWARD		
			Best American	Best Foreign	Best Play
1977	Michael Cristofer *The Shadow Box*	Michael Cristofer *The Shadow Box*	David Mamet *American Buffalo*	No Award	Simon Gray *Otherwise Engaged*
1978	Donald L. Coburn *The Gin Game*	Hugh Leonard *Da*	Hugh Leonard *Da*		
1979	Sam Shepard *Buried Child*	Bernard Pomerance *The Elephant Man*	Bernard Pomerance *The Elephant Man*		
1900	Lanford Wilson *Talley's Folly*	Mark Medoff *Children of a Lesser God*	No Award	Harold Pinter *Betrayal*	Lanford Wilson *Talley's Folly*
1981	Beth Henley *Crimes of the Heart*	Peter Shaffer *Amadeus*	Beth Henley *Crimes of the Heart*	No Award	Athol Fugard *A Lesson from Aloes*
1982	Charles Fuller *A Soldier's Play*	David Edgar *The Life and Adventures of Nicholas Nickleby*	Charles Fuller *A Soldier's Play*	No Award	David Edgar *The Life and Adventures of Nicholas Nickleby*
1983	Marsha Norman *Night, Mother*	Harvey Fierstein *Torch Song Trilogy*	No Award	David Hare *Plenty*	Neil Simon *Brighton Beach Memoirs*
1984	David Mamet *Glengarry Glen Ross*	Tom Stoppard *The Real Thing*	David Mamet *Glengarry Glen Ross*	No Award	Tom Stoppard *The Real Thing*
1985	Stephen Sondheim, music/lyrics James Lapine, book *Sunday in the Park with George*	Neil Simon *Biloxi Blues*	**August Wilson** ***Ma Rainey's Black Bottom***		
1986	No Award	Herb Gardener *I'm Not Rappaport*	Michael Frayn *Benefactors*	No Award	Sam Shepard *A Lie of the Mind*

	PULITZER PRIZE	TONY AWARD	NY DRAMA CRITICS CIRCLE AWARD		
			Best American	Best Foreign	Best Play
1987	August Wilson *Fences*	August Wilson *Fences*	No Award	Christopher Hampton *Les Liaisons Dangereuses*	August Wilson *Fences*
1988	Alfred Uhry *Driving Miss Daisy*	David Henry Hwang *M. Butterfly*	No Award	Athol Fugard *Road to Mecca*	August Wilson *Joe Turner's Come and Gone*
1989	Wendy Wasserstein *The Heidi Chronicles*	Wendy Wasserstein *The Heidi Chronicles*	No Award	Brian Friel *Aristocrats*	Wendy Wasserstein *The Heidi Chronicles*
1990	August Wilson *The Piano Lesson*	Frank Galati *The Grapes of Wrath*	No Award	Peter Nichols *Privates on Parade*	August Wilson *The Piano Lesson*
1991	Neil Simon *Lost in Yonkers*	Neil Simon *Lost in Yonkers*	No Award	Timberlake Wertenbaker *Our Country's Good*	John Guare *Six Degrees of Separation*
1992	Robert Schenkkan *The Kentucky Cycle*	Brian Friel *Dancing at Lughnasa*	August Wilson *Two Trains Running*	No Award	Brian Friel *Dancing at Lughnasa*
1993	Tony Kushner *Angels in America: Millennium Approaches*	Tony Kushner *Angels in America: Millennium Approaches*	No Award	Frank McGuinness *Someone Who'll Watch Over Me*	Tony Kushner *Angels in America: Millennium Approaches*
1994	Edward Albee *Three Tall Women*	Tony Kushner *Angels in America: Perestroika*	Edward Albee *Three Tall Women*		
1995	Horton Foote *The Young Man From Atlanta*	Terrence McNally *Love! Valour! Compassion!*	Terrence McNally *Love! Valour! Compassion!*	No Award	Tom Stoppard *Arcadia*
1996	Jonathan Larson *Rent*	Terrence McNally *Master Class*	No Award	Brian Friel *Molly Sweeney*	August Wilson *Seven Guitars*
1997	No Award	Alfred Uhry *The Last Night of Ballyhoo*	No Award	David Hare *Skylight*	Paula Vogel *How I Learned to Drive*

	PULITZER PRIZE	TONY AWARD	NY DRAMA CRITICS CIRCLE AWARD		
			Best American	Best Foreign	Best Play
1998	Paula Vogel *How I Learned to Drive*	Yasmina Reza *Art*	Tina Howe *Pride's Crossing*	No Award	Yasmina Reza *Art*
1999	Margaret Edson *Wit*	Warren Leight *Side Man*	No Award	Patrick Marber *Closer*	Margaret Edson *Wit*
2000	Donald Margulies *Dinner with Friends*	Michael Frayn *Copenhagen*	No Award	Michael Frayn *Copenhagen*	**August Wilson** ***Jitney***
2001	David Auburn *Proof*	David Auburn *Proof*	David Auburn *Proof*	No Award	Tom Stoppard *The Invention of Love*
2002	Suzan-Lori Parks *Topdog/Underdog*	Edward Albee *The Goat: or, Who Is Sylvia?*	Edward Albee *The Goat: or, Who Is Sylvia?*		
2003	Nilo Cruz *Anna in the Tropics*	Richard Greenburg *Take Me Out*	No Award	Alan Bennett *Talking Heads*	Richard Greenburg *Take Me Out*
2004	Doug Wright *I Am My Own Wife*	Doug Wright *I Am My Own Wife*	Lynn Nottage *Intimate Apparel*		
2005	John Patrick Shanley *Doubt, a Parable*	John Patrick Shanley *Doubt, a Parable*	No Award	Martin McDonagh *The Pillowman*	John Patrick Shanley *Doubt, a Parable*
2006	No Award	Alan Bennet *The History Boys*	Alan Bennett *The History Boys*		
2007	David Lindsay-Abaire *Rabbit Hole*	Tom Stoppard *The Coast of Utopia*	**August Wilson** ***Radio Gulf***	No Award	Tom Stoppard *The Coast of Utopia*

INDEX

The entries in the index include highlights from the main In an Hour essay portion of the book.

ABOUT THE AUTHOR

Dr. Joan Herrington is a contemporary theater scholar whose research is focused on the pedagogy and practice of theater in the last twenty years. She is the author of four books that examine the creative process of playwrights and directors. She has also written a dozen books, chapters, and journal articles appearing in *Journal of Dramatic Theory and Criticism*, *American Drama*, and *The Drama Review*. She has served as editor of the prestigious publication, *Theatre Topics*. Through her research and practice, she has explored modern theater around the world and engaged theater artists from Japan to Great Britain to Nigeria.

Dr. Herrington has taught workshops at many universities. Her work as a director has taken her from coast to coast with productions in New York and Los Angeles, and as far as the Edinburgh Festival in Scotland.

Dr. Herrington is well known for her scholarship on August Wilson whom she met in the summer of 1984 at the Eugene O'Neill Theatre Center. She found him an extraordinary man who intrigued her with his creative process, inspired her with his poetry, and shared with her his glad heart. She is grateful for their years of friendship.

Smith and Kraus would like to thank Dutton Signet, a division of Penguin Group (USA), Inc. and Theatre Communications Group, whose enlightened permissions policies reflect an understanding that copyright law is intended to both protect the rights of creators of intellectual property as well as to encourage its use for the public good.

Know the playwright,
love the play.

Open a new door to theater study, performance, and audience satisfaction with these Playwrights In an Hour titles.

ANCIENT GREEK

Aeschylus Aristophanes Euripides Sophocles

RENAISSANCE

William Shakespeare

MODERN

Anton Chekhov Noël Coward Lorraine Hansberry
Henrik Ibsen Arthur Miller Molière Eugene O'Neill
Arthur Schnitzler George Bernard Shaw August Strindberg
Frank Wedekind Oscar Wilde Thornton Wilder
Tennessee Williams

CONTEMPORARY

Edward Albee Alan Ayckbourn Samuel Beckett
Theresa Rebeck Sarah Ruhl Sam Shepard Tom Stoppard
August Wilson

To purchase or for more information
visit our web site inanhourbooks.com

h